DATE DUE

	AUG 1 2 2004		
			Demco

★ FALLING HARD ★

★ FALLING HARD ★

★ A ROOKIE'S YEAR IN BOXING ★

CHRIS JONES

Arcade Publishing • New York

FIRST U.S. EDITION 2002

First published in 2001 by House of Anansi Press Limited, Canada

ISBN 1-55970-621-X
Libarary of Congress Control Number 2001134053
Library of Congress Cataloging-in-Publication information is available.

Published in the United States by Arcade Publishing, Inc., New York
Distributed by AOL Time Warner Book Group

Visit our Web site at www.arcadepub.com

10 9 8 7 6 5 4 3 2 1

Designed by Bill Douglas at The Bang

EB

PRINTED IN THE UNITED STATES OF AMERICA

For Mo and Do,
the best corner a kid could have

★ CONTENTS ★

PROLOGUE

My boxing story, like all others, starts with a lucky break.

It was early 1998. I was about to finish a degree in urban planning. Blueprints of highways and shopping malls had already lost their appeal, however, and on a bit of a whim, I decided journalism was a superior option. Key friends conspired to sit me down in front of Ken Whyte, the then editor of *Saturday Night* magazine. The meeting represented my first lesson as a would-be reporter: journalism is founded almost exclusively on contacts.

Contacts or not, breaking into the game can be tougher than eight rounds in jungle heat. But for reasons unknown to me — gut instinct, a touch of heartburn — Ken gave me a shot. Just not with *Saturday Night*. My future, Ken told me, was in newspapers, and I was to work for the *National Post*. Thing is, it didn't yet exist. It wouldn't go to press, with Ken taking the helm, until the end of October. In the meantime, I had to bone up on my new profession.

I spent the summer learning how to write broadsheet-style at a news bureau, churning out stories that resembled binary code. Smokes and column inches can make anyone look hard up, but it was a difficult apprenticeship — trial by wire. I fumbled my way through each day, learning something new about municipal politics and mutual funds and the revolution in Muzak, but never wrapping my head around deadline's formula. I questioned my life's new direction. Self-doubt crept in.

My insecurity was furthered by gossip's sharpshooters. Ken had hired a corps of young reporters like me, and we were all stationed at the bureau, a gang of amateurs in need of coaching. It didn't take long for a few disgruntled veterans to label us Ken's Kids. Our mistakes were quick to make the watercooler rounds, and a bad fit was made worse. Half of me wanted to quit. The other half was tempted to agree.

Never mind. I climbed aboard the embryonic *Post* when autumn finally arrived and landed a place in the sports department. I was ecstatic with my job title: sportswriter. And I was sparked by the excitement around the birth of the paper. Opening night saw me fully rejuvenated. I felt cocky for the first time in a long while, as though the world was at my feet.

At twenty-five, I was one of the youngest reporters in the newsroom, a green kid with good fortune to burn. I should have been satisfied for the moment, but in my mind, my journey was not complete. I was a year older than Norman Mailer when he wrote *The Naked and the Dead*. I needed to make up for lost time. Make a name for myself. Ambition, fuelled by a desire to stick it to my critics, began to surface.

Graham Parley, the sports editor, encouraged my ascent. Though he wasn't especially thrilled to welcome me — Ken had fought to find a place for me at the paper — he became my champion soon enough. I first earned Graham's trust when he asked me to write a feature on hockey icon Don Cherry and I found a good story. It was my inaugural visit to the section's front page. A step closer to a good place.

I needed to secure my foothold. I needed to make a second hit. Not surprisingly, the sports that grabbed headlines were taken by senior writers. But one day, while I was sifting through what remained uncovered, a television in the newsroom clicked to a fight. I watched it unfold. Its rhythm made me bounce in my chair. I began to care about the outcome. By the sixth round, pennies and fighters had dropped. Boxing. It was unloved and unclaimed, the abandoned child on the department's stoop.

My plan had a single flaw: boxing had never had a hold on me. I had a passing interest in the game and watched the occasional money fight, but, as is true for most men, boxing occupied a peripheral part of my imagination. It seemed distant, lurking in a hard, dark world behind one of those peepholes that bouncers slide open to demand to know who's knocking.

But I had a press pass, I told myself, and bouncers didn't mean shit to me. A press pass. The key to unlocking secrets and skirting roadblocks. A rectangular piece of laminated white paper with PRESS across the top in bold block letters. It also bore my photograph. My autograph. Graham's stamp of approval in blue ink.

It looked basic as I spun it in my hands, one notch above homemade. No matter. Consider, two years later, where it's taken me: face to face with Don King, within a breath of Mike Tyson, to Muhammad Ali's birthday party. Ringside at the heavyweight championship of the world. I decided then that I owned a ticket to a universe that would let me steal its riches, sap its energy, and transmit it to the page. The sweet science has long turned paupers into heroes. I would be next in line.

For a moment, I savoured an instant of naive clarity. I believed I was on my way to the top, set to follow in great footsteps. Little did I realize. My fall had just begun.

AUTHOR'S NOTE

Rather than confuse matters by using the full names of boxing's sanctioning bodies in the text, I have included only their acronyms.

There are four widely recognized organizations in boxing, each of which awards its own titles and sanctions its own champions. It makes for a bit of an alphabet soup, and there are constant calls for reform and consolidation. They are never heeded.

The World Boxing Council (WBC) is the oldest and therefore least progressive organization, but its belts are generally considered the most prestigious, particularly among heavyweights. The International Boxing Federation (IBF) was established later as a boxer-friendly organization, but it has since become as reviled as the others. The World Boxing Association (WBA) falls somewhere in between, at least in my mind.

Slightly below the three senior organizations — which combine to crown unified champions only when a single boxer holds all three belts, a rare event — is the World Boxing Organization (WBO). It is regarded as a second-tier sanctioning body, but some good fighters are loyal to its ranks.

In my humble opinion, boxing would be better off without any of them.

While we're on the subject of acronyms, a KO, in its most devastating form, is a stone-cold knockout, ten seconds of darkness in the closed eyes of the victim. A TKO, or technical knockout, is slightly less brutal: it occurs when one boxer is on his feet but unsteady, and the referee declares him unfit to continue the bout. Either way, the loser is left with some kind of headache.

★ 1 ★

ALL WISHES GRANTED BUT ONE

★ OTIS GRANT V. ROY JONES JR. ★

NOVEMBER 14, 1998

Like Melville's ocean, or Twain's Mississippi, boxing calls to a young man. Its victims are not only those who forfeit their wits and dive into the ring. The sport seduces writers, too, dragging them down with its powerful undertow of testosterone. Many die a hideous literary death, drowning in their own hyperbole. Only a few — Ernest Hemingway, Jimmy Cannon, A. J. Liebling — cross to safety. Awash in all that blood, they become more buoyant.

— J. R. MOEHRINGER, "RESURRECTING THE CHAMP"

A WHITE TOWEL

Otis Grant finds himself flat on his back for the second time. A sonic surge washes from the cheap seats over the sportswriters at ringside, making it hard for us to think. White blood cells rush to mend eardrums that vibrate in panic, like fish electrocuted during a lightning storm.

Fuck me, it's loud.

Roy Jones Jr., the champion, seems unimpressed with the ovation but pleased with his handiwork. He glides to a neutral corner. A smirk crosses his face, and his gold trunks flash under the hot lights. Grant, the challenger, opens his eyes and wonders why he can't see. (The reason: a solid right, one of many significant blows sustained during the fight.) But instinct takes hold. He draws his knees to his chest, forces himself to exhale, climbs to his feet, and bounces at the ready.

"Everything okay?" the referee asks with seemingly genuine concern. Grant nods as though he's a drunk driver who's been asked whether he's sober. Guts, not brains, give permission for the rest of his body to absorb still more punishment. The referee signals that the fight will continue. I am amazed. The other writers look uninterested. I wonder if they are acting, if they have learned to swallow emotion.

Ten rounds ago, Grant entered the ring to reggae's beats. He wore a black satin robe with the Canadian maple leaf on one sleeve and Jamaica's green and gold bands on the other. His corner included Russ Anber, his long-time manager and confidant; Howard Grant, his older brother; and Dewith Frazer, a former Jamaican champion and proprietor of the Jamestown Boxing Club outside Toronto.

Cut man Bob Miller, his hands filled with swabs and grease, rounded out the crew.

It was the ever-loyal Anber, spit bucket in hand, who led the camp to the apron. A white towel was draped over his shoulder. He looked worried. His eyes darted about the makeshift arena, which hours before had been the bingo hall at the Foxwoods Resort Casino in Mashantucket, Connecticut. Earlier that same evening, the place had been filled with blue-haired people with hearts too faint for craps. Blotters were now exchanged for blood.

In the days prior to the fight, Anber had driven cigarettes into his mouth with chest-breaking regularity. Outwardly, the nicotine established a frantic cadence, but the smokes helped calm the teacher before he sent his favourite pupil to battle. "Roy Jones is the best in the world pound for pound," Anber admitted. "We know we have a monumental task in front of us. We've trained hard. We're ready. We're professional. We're going to give it our best shot. But we know it's going to take our best and a little bit more." Jones boasted a record of 37–1 with 31 knockouts. Anber hoped Grant would not be number 32.

Jones boldly followed Grant into the ring, accompanied by a massive entourage and his own rap music at a violent volume. The crowd had given the Canadian visitor a surprisingly rousing cheer, but its loyalties were made clear when Jones shimmied to the beat and began to strut. The building expanded in response, the way a bull does when it bursts from a rodeo chute. I gripped the table rattling in front of me as the air was sucked out of my lungs. I thought I was going to be crushed by the sensation. Implosion by ovation.

My first fight. Three rows of writers pen me in. Michael Katz, who acts as though he's the dean of the New York press gang, separates me from the ring. He's a squat man with an immense head, made larger by a poor-boy cap and a neck brace. Sitting behind Katz is like sitting behind a helmetless astronaut whose cranium seeks to fill the vacuum. Behind me sits a man who looks like a professor at a northeastern university. I recognize him as Thomas Hauser, biographer to Muhammad Ali and a writer of no small renown.

Bookended by legends, I feel completely out of place.

The media pack begins banging out massacre headlines, the wires predict disaster, and the opening bell hasn't even been rung. Jones is the heavy, heavy favourite. He has demolished all comers within the light-heavyweight division. (His one loss came via disqualification, when Jones knocked out an opponent who had fallen to his knees.) Grant, on the other hand, has come up from the middleweight ranks to make the fight. Though skilled, he is a relative unknown outside boxing's tight circle. The fat guys who matter don't give Grant a chance. Murder looms.

Like a dying man giving up the struggle, I surrender to the atmosphere. It pours into me and eases my sense of dread. Waitresses in short boxing robes ply the crowd with booze. Sports celebrities — including Patrick Ewing and seven members of the New England Patriots — find their platinum-plated seats. Holy shit, I think, as I scan the crowd. That's Magic Johnson. Autograph hounds hog the floor around him. Bad characters flash gaudy jewels and gold teeth. Gangbangers make arcane symbols with their hands. The air is thick with liquor and sweat. I breathe it in and try not to choke.

My pupils dilate, and my throat is dry. My hands tremble above my keyboard, shaking with excitement and fear. Come on, Otis, make these motherfuckers eat their words. Come on.

Anber gives Grant a couple of smacks on the ass before the two boxers touch gloves. The bell sounds. Jones and Grant test each other only slightly during the opening round. Few punches are thrown, fewer punches are taken. But Grant suffers one smart jab to his left eye, a Buckley's Mixture taste of the barrage to come.

Miller applies a cold compress to the eye between rounds. Anber dances in front of Grant: "To the left," he counsels. "Move to the goddamn left." But Jones is too fast, and he takes the next two frames handily. Grant's eye begins to swell and turn an unhealthy colour. Jones hears cries of "Showtime!" rise repeatedly from his animated corner. The champ is compelled to go in for the kill.

In the fourth round, he obliges. Jones catches Grant with a vicious right to the head. It's enough to stagger the underdog. Grant stumbles across the canvas. He teeters. The crowd senses an end and takes to its feet. But Grant somehow stays on his. Jones then misses with an uppercut, a black flash that would have ended the fight had it found the mark. Last seconds tick away. The bell rings with mercy. At the break, Anber tells Grant he can't take a punch like that again.

Grant responds to the challenge in the fifth round. He goes on the offensive for the first time. He said before the fight that he'd start slowly but then open things up. The latter part of his strategy finally materializes. A flustered Jones tries to match the left-handed Grant. He fights as a southpaw for part of the round — is he scared? tired? — but he soon assumes his more usual stance. Grant unloads a flurry of punches at the close of the round. A few of them land.

First the bell. Then comes the sixth.

Jones decides to conclude matters with a punishing left. It catches Grant hard. The punch distorts his face with pain and shock. He trips over backward and rolls to the canvas, his knees pulled up to his chest. Again the crowd stands. The guy sitting behind Magic Johnson can't see a damn thing. Anber looks ill, ready to faint. Worst fears have come true.

But Grant climbs to his feet, and Jones resumes the assault. The bridge of Grant's nose is cut. His cheek begins to darken into a deep bruise. Perhaps a second too late, the round comes to a close. Grant needs the ropes to find his corner. Anber talks to his fighter; his fighter wants to press on, to go the distance.

The seventh round is devoid of action. The eighth is a little better. Still, the bloodhounds in the bleachers begin to protest. Their outrage sickens me. I want the fight over.

The ninth round, however, is Grant's strongest by far. He goes on the offensive again and lands a couple of lefts and a combination. Jones looks surprised and begins to miss punches. A man in the crowd yells, "Attack, Otis, attack!" Grant obeys and wins the

CP PICTURE ARCHIVE (Matt York)

★★OTIS GRANT
STRUGGLES NOT TO LOSE
HIS HEAD AGAINST THE FORMIDABLE
ROY JONES JR.

frame. A buzz cuts through the arena: No way . . . Jones can't lose . . . Impossible. I am flushed with belief. I am about to witness history, an epic upset.

To the tenth. First, Jones throws a hard right. Grant falls. "Everything okay?" the referee asks after Grant jumps to his feet once again. Grant nods sluggishly. He looks ready to work. Ready to throw himself back into the fray. The referee indicates that business remains unfinished. When from Grant's corner comes a towel.

Anber's white towel. It travels from his shoulder to the centre of the ring. The referee looks stunned. Throwing in the towel is forbidden in Connecticut. The referee kicks the offending object out of the ring and orders the boxers to come together.

But through the ropes steps Anber. The referee complains. Anber explains there will not be a knockout on his watch and shrugs. He embraces Grant. There is no final bell.

The crowd heaps abuse upon the vanquished before it celebrates the success of its hero. Bangers storm the ringside cameras in a futile attempt for airtime. "East Coast!" they yell until their stomachs begin to bleed.

Fuck me, it's loud.

IN THIS CORNER

Shortly after I decide to hitch a ride on boxing's coattails, I catch wind of this Otis Grant–Roy Jones Jr. fight. I don't know anything about Grant, because I don't know much about boxing. But he holds a Canadian passport, which is enough to pique my interest, and I've heard of Jones, so I know the fight must be a big deal.

The newsroom library holds a collection of old articles on Grant. The files tell a tale I'm only too happy to hear. Grant is the WBO middleweight champion and will have to move up two weight classes to meet Jones, who holds the WBA and WBC light-heavyweight belts. (Instant underdog.) Better yet, he is a

schoolteacher when he isn't in the ring, with a well-earned reputation as a gentleman in a sport of thugs. (Easy angle.) It also seems
the Jamaican-born, Montreal-bred Grant hasn't received the attention he deserves, which is the ribbon on a gift of a story. He
probably has a lot to say.

Russ Anber makes the premise even more perfect. A young
Burgess Meredith, Anber has managed Otis since 1981, when Otis
was thirteen years old and Russ hadn't yet turned twenty. I know
his name from his time spent with the CBC as a commentator.
On the air, he's scrappy but owns a sentimental side. Fiery but a
soft touch. I give him a call, and he's all for my attention.

I pitch the entire package to Graham, who is desperate for
Canadian stories. He agrees we should cover the fight. Grant's
chances are less than nil, but he's challenging for a pair of world
titles. He's news. He's also a rare feel-good story in a do-bad sport.
If he wins, he becomes a pugilistic fairy tale. If he's defeated, he
becomes another broken heart. I can't lose.

I take a taxi to the sportsplex north of Toronto where Russ told me
Otis would be working out. I find it nestled among ware-
houses and strip malls. Past the airport. A fifty-dollar fare from
downtown.

Not knowing what Otis looks like, I walk right past him when
I enter the gym. He's stretched out on a weight bench. A personal
trainer named Billy is kneeling beside him. Billy has been
assigned the task of adding twelve pounds of muscle to Grant's
frame. Trouble is, Billy doesn't seem to like me. And he definitely
doesn't want me watching Otis lift weights. "No offence," he mut-
ters, "but no way." Otis doesn't seem to care, but I decide not to
argue. I don't want my first boxing story to begin with a punch
to my face.

With several hours to kill before watching Otis spar with a
lanky kid named Eric Harding, I venture out to explore the neigh-
bourhood, or at least what passes for one in the suburbs. It's very
cold. I wander around, eyes streaming, fists jammed in pockets,

until I find a dodgy pub, suitably rough to put me in the mood for boxing. Bud from the bottle, a warm meal.

I endeavour to keep my brain as hot as my stomach. I read over a few clippings from Otis's file and try to formulate some decent questions for our interview, which is slated to follow his sparring session. I don't really know how to approach things. I feel as though I know Otis from the stories I've read, and I've already cast him in a sympathetic role. At the same time, I don't want to insult him by suggesting he's out of his league. All fighters must have sizeable egos, or they wouldn't be able to do what they do. The mystery is how to stroke that ego while still extracting something vulnerable from deep within. Do boxers ever experience doubt? I wonder. As I settle up my bill, the first hints of a headache come.

Out in the frigid air again, I make my way to Dewith Frazer's Jamestown Boxing Club, in Unit 7 of another strip mall. A number of the other units are vacant, but near neighbours include the Fish & Bird Emporium, Brew-A-Batch Quality Beer, and Nick's Welding & Fabricating. From the outside, the gym looks like a similar operation, where a marginal living is earned through small sales and stubborn hope. It also looks warm.

Russ sees me walk in with a lost look on my face, figures he's found the right guy, and introduces himself. "Make yourself at home," he says. I try to appear knowledgeable as I poke around before settling into a chair in a corner of the club.

The place is made of cinderblock. A massive mural of Sugar Ray Leonard fighting Roberto Duran, as far as I can tell, covers one wall. The other walls are all fight posters and mirrors. Heavy bags wrapped with duct tape dangle at the bottom of chains. Speed bags hang low from the ceiling. There's a weight bench and a single, small ring.

Dewith Frazer surveys his domain. He appears to be a proud man. "I have broad shoulders," he smiles, and this seems to say it all. His office, just down the hall from the ring and across from the toilet, is packed with souvenirs acquired over a long tenure in the sport.

Otis arrives from the locker room and wants to begin his routine, but a TV crew has set up shop. Russ whispers in Otis's ear and he does his time for TV. After a few questions, he begins his workout. The crew leaves. It's down to me and the camp.

Otis's workout is precise and refined. It has the irresistible force of habit, with carefully measured stints of skipping and jabbing and sparring. Eric, who has a couple of inches on Otis, does well during the eight rounds of padded brawling. He's an awkward opponent — quick, with a long reach. Russ, who sits with me while the fighters shower, tells me Otis will be much better by the time he fights Jones.

When the freshly scrubbed Otis appears, we adjourn to Frazer's office. Behind closed doors, Otis settles into one of the eight meals he downs daily in an effort to gain weight.

He doesn't sit in his chair so much as he drapes himself over it, his food in his lap, his feet spread apart. Russ is more erect, professional for the imaginary cameras. In different ways, both of them try to keep their nerves from surfacing. Otis has an air of relaxation, Russ carries decorum's shield. Neither technique works. The fight is clearly weighing heavily on both their minds.

I decide not to ask about Jones for the time being. We talk instead about Otis and Russ — how they met, how they work, how they manage to stay close in a business known for its quickly severed ties. "He's like family now," Otis says simply, in between bites of chicken and cauliflower that fill his cheeks. The tightest of bonds can be made in a beat-up van, driving to nickel-and-dime fights in Atlantic City and Boston and South Carolina. The thought pleases me. It's good stuff for the story. It'll be easy to convince readers to root for Otis.

I find myself onside as well. Otis, prompted by Russ, talks about his university education and his work as a counsellor for troubled high-school kids. About his wife, Betty, who was his high-school sweetheart. About his beloved daughter, Alexandria. It's almost too perfect, sweet like syrup, but I continue to write down quotes as the tape recorder spins with gold.

Yet something nags at me. Otis laughs during our conversation, his face creasing and his broad nose crinkling, but his eyes remain unsmiling and distant. He doesn't blink as often as he should, as though he's deep in thought. I feel like I never quite have his attention. And as I continue to pry, Russ becomes jittery. "You got what you need, Chris?" he asks. I look at him and sense a secret is about to leak out. Perhaps an admission of fear.

There is time for one final question, a backdoor approach. I ask Otis why he fights when he doesn't have to. The Jones fight presents him with his biggest payday, he begins — $400,000 US, four times more than his previous fight. Of course, Jones stands to make millions, blowing apart the risk-reward theory of economics, but for Otis the fight remains "the opportunity of a lifetime." For Alexandria, too. His voice dips especially low, and an important truth comes: "I do it," says Otis, "for her."

He makes a fast break out of his reflective stance, his eyes flickering to life once again and becoming bright with bravado. "He's a great fighter," Otis says of Jones. "I'm not going to go on record saying I'm going to beat him or knock him out. But if I fight the way I can fight, it will be a very competitive fight, much more so than people think." It sounds as though he's convinced himself, and the three of us rise to leave.

After the interview, Otis climbs into an ancient hatchback with Eric and Billy, laughing and joking. They're like a group of kids heading for a concert. They seem far removed from violence as they peel happily out of the parking lot.

While I stand in the cold waiting for a taxi, I notice a poster taped to the window in the gym's front door. It's for a 1994 Roy Jones Jr. fight and proclaims him one of the best fighters of the 1990s. I shake my head — not with disbelief, but with worry. I feel like I've pledged allegiance to a losing cause.

The next time I see the camp is at Foxwoods. I fly into Providence, Rhode Island, via Philadelphia — Fight Town — and take a shuttle to the resort.

Foxwoods is a massive Indian operation, reputed to house the world's largest casino. A haven for badness. There is a single, gigantic hotel that looks like a faux Bavarian castle, bordered by a couple of smaller inns. Five million square feet of real estate. Beyond the buildings stretch miles of thick woods. People arrive here by the busload, camp out for a week, and do nothing but gamble. It's a factory built to extract money. And there's no escape: Foxwoods is more secure than a prison. Smack in the middle of the Connecticut wilderness, the casino's slot machines drown out the chirps of birds. The stock of one retail stall in the complex consists largely of pain-relief remedies.

The pre-fight press conference provides a much-needed respite. Jones arrives with his promoter, Murad Muhammad, a cross between a low-rent Don King and Louis Farrakhan. I sit with a few writers from Montreal, and Otis and Russ join us. They're minor figures in the ongoing drama that is the life of Roy Jones Jr. Muhammad even forgets Russ's name when he introduces the participants. Otis was a third choice for HBO, the US television giant that finances most major fights, and he has been widely dismissed by the American press. I put it down to national ego, but the arrogance pisses me off. Bias secures itself in my psyche.

"You have to understand there were a lot of people who were against the fight," says Otis's promoter, an excitable Philadelphian named Art Pelullo. "A lot of people didn't believe it was a credible match," he continues, with the whine of someone who was beaten up a lot in high school. "They didn't understand what a quality fighter Otis Grant is."

Jones, dressed in sweats and sandals, is clearly treating the fight as a charity match rather than a boxing event. "Otis is a guy who deserves credibility," he says. "He deserves an opportunity. He deserves a great payday. Why not help some of the good people in this sport?" Jones seems bored as well as magnanimous, and he talks about retirement. He'll knock out Otis first, but he doesn't seem excited about the prospect. "It's hard," Jones admits, "when you don't hate the other guy." Give me a break. Even Jones likes Otis.

But behind the love is mean intent. Before and after the press conference, footage of some of Jones's more brutal knockouts is projected onto giant video screens. In one of the fights, Jones knocks out Virgil Hill — no chump — with a right hand to the kidney, not to the head. Hill crumples to the canvas and curls into a ball. He presses his glove to his burning side. A stunned George Foreman sits at ringside: "I've seen it all," he says.

If I were Otis, I'd be looking for an excuse not to show up.

Otis, however, doesn't seem fazed by the display. "I've seen all the tapes before," he says. "I'm not going into this fight in awe of Roy Jones. I'm going into this fight like it's another fight. When all the hype settles, it will be just me and him and the referee in the ring. He's got two arms, I've got two arms. He's got two legs, I've got two legs." Russ, smoke pouring from his face, looks a little more concerned.

I head to the weigh-in the next day after an evening of gambling alone. The Montreal writers had gone out for dinner together before hitting the tables, but I wasn't invited. I'm not sure if it's because I'm young or because I'm new, but I decide to keep my distance at the morning physical. I'm better off without them. "Losers," I tell myself.

Jones is the first to take to the scale in a room filled with the flattened noses and protruding brows of the fourteen fighters on the card. He weighs in at 171 pounds. Otis then climbs aboard, looking fit and filled out. Murad Muhammad yells, "185 pounds!" to those assembled. In reality, Otis is exactly 172 pounds, the upper weight limit for his bout with Jones. (The regulation light-heavyweight limit is 175 pounds, but Jones agreed to drop a little weight to make the fight more fair.) Otis has done his part. He's passed the first test, and his physique makes the fight credible.

But a weigh-in, I gather from eavesdropping on conversations between more educated analysts, is a deceptive display. Fighters can apparently cut huge amounts of weight in a few hours, jump on the scale, and pack on the pounds again afterward. Jones, claims one reporter, can shed and gain fifteen pounds with ease. As if to prove the point, he tucks into an entire roast chicken after the weigh-in — Otis heads for the hotel buffet — and the official weights fast become history. Otis must hope the same won't be said of him.

"He doesn't get recognition for being a college graduate, a schoolteacher, for taking care of his wife and his daughter and his mom," complains Pelullo, who clings to friendly reporters like a puppy. "But if he was a psycho, or whacking out people, or getting three or four broads pregnant, or biting somebody's ear, he'd be all over the news. But none of that matters now. No matter what happens, Otis becomes a bigger player after this fight."

Yes, I agree. Me, too.

THE LIGHTS BEGIN TO GO OUT

Saturday night. I have never before attended a professional fight. I feel upbeat but anxious. I have somehow convinced myself that Otis will win. Russ, Dewith, Billy, Art, and Eric, they all say this kid Grant shouldn't be underestimated. Never mind that Jones has destroyed everybody he's ever fought: "Forget about it, smart guy. Just put your money on Otis." I throw in my compassion for good measure. Not a wise move, I have sense enough to realize. Perhaps I should have heeded the green signs that litter the casino walls at Foxwoods: "Bet with your head, not with your heart. Gamble wisely."

The press room is packed. A buffet dinner is served. Steaming heaps of food and a rain barrel of ice and drinks are presented to us. Now I see why most sportswriters are fat. Reporters also get a loot bag when credentials are confirmed. A T-shirt. A coffee mug. A restaurant coupon. Nothing like a little graft to start the evening.

Like a basement bar, the place is alight with gossip and predictions. The consensus: Otis Grant will be decapitated. I sit with the *Globe and Mail*'s Stephen Brunt and Steve Buffery of the

Toronto Sun. Brunt is regarded as the best sportswriter in Canada, but he's too friendly for me to begrudge him. Buffery also makes me feel like part of the gang. He's welcoming and quick to crack wise. Sportswriters are turning out to be a collegial bunch, the Montreal reporters excepted. They eye the Toronto contingent with suspicion, still harbouring a thing about Upper Canadians. But with appetites satisfied and predictions made, we all find our way to the converted bingo hall. My stomach begins to churn while the grandstands fill.

The crowd looks tough, on the edge of volatile. Mashantucket lays claim to a place in boxing's hinterland. No one happens to be there. A man who makes the trip must love fights, and to love fights is to hold something dark inside. The air inside the arena actually looks black, as though it has depth or possesses the properties of water. I feel like an aquanaut, laboured and slow-moving.

We find our submerged seats. Michael Katz has already found his place and seems intent on blocking my view. I set up my computer on the table in front of me, open up a notepad, and wait for the Main Event. The *National Post* doesn't publish on Sundays, so I face no deadline pressure, and I scratch down first impressions without bringing my eyes to the paper. I don't want to miss anything. I also try to tie myself down, keep myself underwhelmed. It isn't easy. There is nothing, I discover during the undercard bouts, like a fight in the flesh. At ringside, I could hear the connections first-hand, and the sound is worse than the sight. Thump. Crack. Buguda. The instructions from corners are loud and clear. As are the unique conversations between boxers. ("You ain't nuthin' to me!") TV refines a raw spectacle. Filters out the brutality.

I can taste the violence, feel it like rain. Sweat splashes over the people who sit too close to the apron, and the ringside photographers all carry towels to wipe their lenses clean between rounds. The occasional dash of blood also squirts over the ropes, staining expensive suits and innocence.

After six undercard fights, Foxwoods has all the atmosphere of a slaughterhouse. Every underdog has lost, has been moved rapidly from the list of contenders to the list of pretenders. (Sizzlin') Sam Girard on points. Tom (The Ripper) Cameron by knockout in the third. (He entered to the strains of a Judas Priest tune and left on the verge of a last-rites vigil.) Darroll (Doin' Damage) Wilson by knockout in the fourth. Luis (The Louisville Slugger) Leija by TKO in the sixth. Tim (The Bear) Hillie on points. (Jesse) James Leija by TKO after nine. Non-stop carnage. I feel like I've seen enough, but only now is it time for the real deal. The TV lights are turned up to full glare. HBO's cameras are rolling. And George Foreman beams at ringside, his microphone at the ready. He wants to see Jones explode another man's kidney or perhaps dent his head. If you could actually cave someone's head in, I get the sense boxing fans would talk about that for a long time to come.

I need a drink. I summon a Foxwoods bunny, all of whom look as though they've gone a few rounds themselves. The bunny wrestles her way within earshot and a warmish beer is soon before me. A mixed drink would be more stylish, but I lack the focus to enjoy a cocktail. I need something more basic. I order another and down it quickly.

At last, Otis Grant makes his way to the ring. He's followed by Roy Jones Jr. I hope to keep the sound of the erupting crowd as a memento by holding my tape recorder in the air. (I play it back later and it sounds like the ocean.) The same noise is produced in the fourth round when Otis is staggered; in the sixth when he falls for the first time; in the tenth when he falls for the second time; and again when the white towel drops to the canvas and Jones is declared the winner.

I am stunned in the end, and not only because it seems I can no longer hear.

TOO CLOSE

There is danger when you get too close to a story: judgement can be clouded, and hearts can be broken. I've grown to like Otis Grant and Russ Anber too much for my own good. No longer a reporter, I've become something of a fan, and that's unfortunate for any number of reasons.

I banked on Otis's becoming world champion. Objectivity, I soon realize, has been the first casualty of my first fight. Otis was the underdog, the Canadian, the polite man, the good father, the teacher. The hero of a tear-jerker. Russ was the hero's big-hearted sidekick. The pairing was thick with loveable stereotype, and it made me soft. I have written a happy ending I'll have to erase.

After the fight, the press gathers in a curtained-off chunk of the bingo hall foyer. Groups of fans have also made it past security. The place is hot, loud, utterly chaotic. I'm fortunate to have a seat, but I'm still dizzy from the crush, wondering how I've ended up in this madhouse. In time, Roy Jones appears with Murad Muhammad, and the two men take their places behind the dais. Both smile broadly. Jones is entirely unmarked. He doesn't even look winded.

Otis joins the circus later, Russ still by his side. They needed time to put themselves back together. Otis is wearing a hat like Jughead's from the *Archie* comics, though a balaclava would have been more appropriate. His face has been picked apart, and time has allowed the damage to surface. He's carpeted with cherry blotches and blemishes. His good nature remains intact, but he has earned his purse.

I feel ashamed when I catch myself staring at Otis, his deep wounds on display for the cameras. Russ, who looks shattered, makes me feel worse. Above the din, he calls out my name. He tries to swallow his disappointment, but it gets lodged somewhere in his throat. I look up and try to smile. Russ holds out his hands and crunches up his shoulders. "What could we do?" his body language says. "We were up against it." I know what he means, and I know everything will be all right. But I'm still upset, cracking like a novice.

The wizened American reporters are interested only in the obvious supremacy of Jones. The room is his. But the Canadians huddle with Otis and Russ, who put on brave faces despite the defeat.

"Why get carried out?" asks Russ. "I'm the godfather of his daughter, and I don't want to assume a responsibility I don't have to. Hey, I'll take the heat. But at least he's going to walk back to his hotel room, wake up tomorrow, take a flight to Montreal, and be in school on Monday."

Otis smiles. "Life goes on," he says. I wonder.

In any sport, losing is tough to take. But now I see how boxing's losers risk permanent damage. Even when a fighter survives defeat, he has still been beaten in the most basic sense. He can find no sanctuary, no comfort. The ring is expressly designed to expose weakness. Flaws are bathed in bright light. Television cameras record every mistake. There is no mask to hide behind, no equipment within which one can disappear. There are only trunks and boots and gloves and two men who risk ending the night in darkness. Almost always at least one of them does. Then comes the dissection. A losing fighter, like most defeated athletes, will say, "Tomorrow is another day." Otis has definitely taken that mantra to heart. But for boxers, tomorrow is when the pain sets in. I know Otis won't really hurt until the morning.

I shake his hand and wish him luck. I'll need some, too. It's almost 2 a.m. before I return to my hotel room and flick on my computer. It casts a blue glow across my dark room. I'm exhausted. The big bed tempts me, but I'm afraid of the dreams headed my way. I turn on a lamp as the casino hums a few floors below, pour myself a soda, and begin to write. I have ten hours before I have to file my first boxing feature. I decide to go upbeat. Work becomes therapy.

"On occasion," I begin, "B-movie plotlines come true."

★ 2 ★

THE WINNER AND STILL HAS-BEEN
★ FRANÇOIS BOTHA V. MIKE TYSON ★
JANUARY 16, 1999

"Badly *cogido*," he said. "All for sport. All for pleasure."

— ERNEST HEMINGWAY, *THE SUN ALSO RISES*

BIG TIME

My piece on Otis Grant appears as a two-page spread in the Monday edition of the *National Post*. My editor loves it. I receive some good mail. Russ calls and says it's "the single most beautiful story" on Otis he's ever read. I feel like I've really made it. Flying on a bit of a high, I decide it's worth doing good work for that feeling alone. As well as the perks that come with success: not long afterward, I'm asked to spend six days in Las Vegas and at week's end watch Mike Tyson — the one-time undisputed heavyweight champion of the world — begin yet another comeback. I've hit the jackpot. Boxing is mine to keep, a sport to call my own.

I waste no time in arranging the trip and set out not a moment too soon. Toronto is about to be hit by a blizzard the morning of my departure. The sky grows dense with threatening clouds, and the taxi ride to the airport takes a long time as the snow has already begun to fall. I narrowly escape. The city is shut down by the storm hours after takeoff; by the time I hear the army has been called in, I'll be under Nevada's sun, having flown to Denver, bought a Colorado croissant at the airport, and boarded the short-hop to Las Vegas. The flight is something of a vomit comet. My seatmate loses it during a bumpy stretch. The odour proves a good warmup for Vegas.

I've visited Sin City once before. It was 1984, and I was eleven years old. My family packed itself into a California-bound station wagon, and Las Vegas served as a pit stop hours short of Los Angeles. I don't remember much about our time there aside from the cheap buffets. And the torrential rain. We were hit good and hard by a desert monsoon. Water rushed down the streets, the neon lights reflected in the rivers. To cross the flooded parking lots of the big casinos, gamblers used overturned shopping carts as stepping stones.

I retrieve those distant memories on the rocky flight from Denver, my mind ticking like ninety despite the acrid smell. I've never been a good flyer, but I manage my best brainwork on planes. The thin air makes me more lucid, and anticipation's adrenaline starts to flow. I envision people all over the world climbing onto planes to converge on a favoured place for one violent purpose: for a fix of the Big Time.

During boxing's high tide, they flew to more exotic locales than dusty Vegas. London. Berlin. Tokyo. Manila. Amazing that people would cross an ocean to watch a scrap. Absorbing, too. I've been reading Norman Mailer's *The Fight*, his famed account of the Ali-Foreman bout held in Zaire in 1974. His descriptions of Kinshasa intrigue me. And make me jealous. It must have seemed as though the world started with the sound of the opening bell.

But Las Vegas will do for now. I fidget in my seat, shaking Africa. Only the view calms me. The sky is cloudless. Mountains and forests give way to canyons and desert. Geography's features become more stark. Thin rivers cut massive valleys. Tiny settlements stick out like thumbtacks on a map. Roads and power lines and dams are made more evident by an uncluttered nature. The lack of vegetation provides fewer places for our ugly things to hide. But there is also goodness. There should be a colour called desert reservoir blue, because water on top of red rock is a uniquely perfect shade, a cross between indigo and hospital green, with a dash of rust thrown in for good measure. There are scars but also beauty marks.

Mike Tyson, however, is bruises and bullet wounds. I read Tyson's file whenever I manage to pull myself away from the window. Each page brings another black mark. From a tender age, Tyson seemed factory-built for boxing.

According to one of the press clippings, the Brooklyn native was arrested as a twelve-year-old in 1978. He had already compiled a long record outside the ring, but his latest purse snatching landed him in the Tryon School for Boys. His brother, whom Tyson repeatedly slashed with a razor during their nights together, was probably relieved. The following year, a boxing instructor at a correctional facility brought Tyson to the attention of Cus D'Amato, a legendary trainer who had guided Floyd Patterson to the heavyweight title. D'Amato made Tyson part of his upstate New York stable. The move did wonders for Tyson as a boxer. But D'Amato spoiled his student and overlooked a series of transgressions that saw Tyson expelled from Catskill High School, and the kid acquired a bully's character. He has never found the straight path, and the only thing narrow about Tyson might be his brainpan.

D'Amato died of pneumonia in 1985, when Tyson was still a teenager. The loss sent the fighter reeling. Any hope for Tyson's redemption was gone for good. But he continued to excel within boxing's ropes. On November 22, 1986, the twenty-year-old Tyson knocked out Trevor Berbick to claim the WBC heavyweight title and become the youngest champion in history. Less than one year later, Tyson was named the undisputed heavyweight champion after he dropped James (Bonecrusher) Smith and Tony Tucker.

Between the moments of glory came still more shame. Tyson developed a reputation for his brutality toward women. He seemed to settle down when he married actress Robin Givens, but she soon filed for divorce after repeated beatings. (Tyson once claimed his best punch was one that sent Givens flying backward, "hitting every fucking wall in the apartment.") Shortly before the couple split, Tyson threw a tantrum — and a considerable amount of furniture through a window at his New Jersey home. Givens and her mother were forced to flee. But women and home interiors were not Tyson's only victims. He was forced to settle out of court after he used a parking attendant to warm up for his fight with Tucker. He engaged in a Harlem street brawl with boxer Mitch Green. And Tyson threatened a reporter and threw his Walkman at a camera crew during a televised fit of rage.

The behaviour finally caught up with Tyson's boxing career. In 1990, he lost his heavyweight title to James (Buster) Douglas in

Japan. Douglas, a diabetic who struggled with his weight, had been a 42–1 underdog. The loss broke Tyson's spell. The man who routinely separated his opponents from their noses was exposed as a fraud. He buckled in the face of adversity, and he simply wasn't scary anymore.

Soon after, Tyson wasn't even boxing anymore. In 1991, he was convicted of the rape of Miss Black America contestant Desiree Washington and was later sentenced to six years in prison. He was released after serving more than three years at an Indiana correctional facility and resumed boxing against a series of tomato cans, of whom Peter McNeeley was the first. Tyson eventually regained his WBC and WBA heavyweight titles after wins over Frank Bruno and Bruce Seldon, but his climb back to stardom came to an abrupt halt at the hands of Evander Holyfield, the philandering prophet.

Holyfield first beat Tyson in November 1996, when the referee stopped the fight in the eleventh round with Iron Mike against the ropes. Their fateful rematch came eight months later. Facing his second straight defeat, Tyson found escape in Holyfield's softest tissue. He twice bit Holyfield's ears, spitting out a chunk of flesh on the canvas shortly before the referee, Mills Lane, ended the fight. Lane disqualified Tyson. Holyfield, one ear less than whole, was declared the winner. Chaos erupted at the MGM Grand, the affair's embarrassed host. Twelve days later, the Nevada State Athletic Commission revoked Tyson's licence to box. It looked to be the end of him, and public opinion was roundly in favour of his permanent exile. I watched Tyson-Holyfield II in a Toronto bar and swore that I'd never again be suckered by boxing. Fortunately, I'm not a religious man and my vows can be undone.

Like me, boxing is nothing if not forgiving, or at least forgetful. Tyson applied for reinstatement after little more than a year's vacation and regained his licence when psychological tests revealed him to be troubled but fit to box. A scant nineteen months after biting Holyfield, Tyson will once again be under the spotlights at the MGM Grand. The Catskill Cashbox has been welcomed back to the fold. There have been howls of protest, but in boxing, money owns the loudest voice.

A lumpy, white South African named François Botha has been selected as Tyson's first post-bite opponent. It's my job to report on their meeting. I scan Tyson's psychological assessment as the desert unfolds below me. It reads in part: "Mr. Tyson's changes from normal mood to anger seem to be triggered by his belief that he is being used, victimized and treated unfairly." I wonder whether Tyson's mood could ever be classified as normal. Botha will no doubt vouch for the anger.

PARADISE MEMORIAL GARDENS

I step out of the arrivals terminal and into the sunshine. A line of taxis awaits. I've decided to visit Sonny Liston's grave before going to my hotel; I'm not certain of its whereabouts, but I know the cemetery is just beyond the airport's runways. I ask the first taxi driver if he knows where Liston now hangs out. "I do," he says, so I climb in.

Along the way, a billboard advertising the Tyson-Botha fight towers above us from the side of the road. It's black and the names of both boxers are stamped across it in white, stark against the bright blue of the Nevada sky. The boxers themselves are pictured back to back. Tyson looks hard and cut. The tattoo of tennis legend Arthur Ashe on his upper left arm is easy to make out, and above it the words "Days of Grace" are inked into Tyson's skin. An apt description for my moment in the sun.

The driver asks why I'm so interested in Sonny Liston, and I tell him I'm in town for the fight. I explain that Tyson often compares himself to boxing's most flawed champion. A graveside visit could provide a useful story device. The driver likes the idea. He talks about the atmosphere of a Las Vegas fight: the hookers, the high-rollers, the gangbangers, the wannabes, the writers — all of them boxing fans for very personal reasons.

Tyson's kinship with Liston, the one-time baddest man in America, was also personal.

Liston never knew where or when he was born. His mother, Helen Baskin, gave birth to a dozen children — Sonny was number twelve — fathered by a sharecropper, Tobe Liston. (The elder Liston was the father of another dozen children by a second woman.) Sonny grew up working in the cotton fields, and he was routinely beaten as a child. He was a street tough in St. Louis by age sixteen; he mugged people, tried his luck at armed robbery, and beat up a cop. Liston went to prison and became a very good professional fighter upon release. He went on to destroy Floyd Patterson and some other men and earned the heavyweight championship, but he was in the Mob's pocket and Americans never loved him. In 1964, Liston was effectively finished by Muhammad Ali (then Cassius Clay). Liston refused to answer the bell at the start of the seventh round. The bully backed down. Not for the last time.

Little else came of Liston until his death. He left for good in 1970. His wife found his body, a needle spiked deep in his arm. Heroin is the accepted cause of his demise, though no one knows who injected the junk. Liston might have been murdered and the drugs used as a decoy. Or Liston himself might have longed for the ultimate escape. Either way, chances are good Liston died on the run. It was a frantic end for a man who essentially ended his boxing career as a statue on a stool.

The image of Liston on his perch is compelling, despair in black and white. Whenever a fighter refuses a stool between rounds — choosing instead to stand with his arms wrapped around the top ropes — he might be thinking of Liston. What could have happened that night in 1964 had Liston not had a stool? He might have continued to fight Ali, scored a lucky punch, and changed boxing history. But Liston sat down. The lactic acid in his legs began to trickle thick through his muscles. The corner acted not as his haven but as quicksand.

The fight blew Liston apart. Only in Las Vegas, only in this traffic jam of a city, could he find tarnished sanctuary. "The history of fighters," writes *New Yorker* editor David Remnick, "is the history of men who end up damaged." Those who tell their stories, Remnick suggests, can't help being affected. I wonder whether I've set myself up for more upset. . . .

The taxi pulls into the cemetery, Paradise Memorial Gardens. It is often in the shadows of planes. Tidy and trim, it's not as big as I expected, and all the gravestones are set into the ground. There are no vertical markers or mausoleums, and there are no signs to direct you toward Liston. Undeterred, the driver asks a groundskeeper where Liston's grave is, and the busy man points at an area of the cemetery called the Garden of Peace. I begin to walk between rows of graves. The driver leans against the car and waits, happy to let his meter tick. I find Liston. He sleeps in an arid purgatory, trapped between an inferno of neon and the runways that afford skyward escape.

The stone on his grave has been blackened by the sun. "Charles 'Sonny' Liston," it reads, "1932–1970. A Man." The date of his birth is a good guess; the epitaph is as perfect as I can imagine. A wilted flower, once pink, lies across the stone's bottom corner. Five American pennies have also been placed on top of it. They, too, have turned black in the heat.

I don't know why, but Liston is buried along the border of the children's section of the cemetery. Small stones have been pressed into the grass where kids named Bobby and James and Grace have been laid to rest. The area is eerily playful. Parents have decorated the graves with stuffed animals and flowers. As I stand before Sonny Liston, pinwheels and balloons dance to my right, their rhythm dictated by jet exhaust. I turn to watch them. Sunlight flashes off the helium-filled foil and into my eyes.

Jim Murray, the late one-eyed columnist for the *Los Angeles Times*, wrote that realizing Liston was the heavyweight champion was like "finding a live bat on a string under your Christmas tree." I walk across the broad-leafed desert grass, climb back into the taxi, and decide that wasn't a decent thing to say about anybody.

LV

The driver drops me off at the MGM Grand. The casino has agreed to play host to Tyson yet again. Twice burned, never shy. Atop the casino rises a massive hotel — 5,005 rooms all told — laid out in the shape of a cross. The elevator shafts occupy the intersection of the two planks. My room is close to Christ's left-hand nail. The room-service trolleys are motorized. The ice machine is an overnight away.

A Sherpa takes me to my door, granting me access to midnight. Hotel rooms in Vegas seem to come with the curtains closed. A nod to discretion. Had I arrived with a hooker and a kilo of blow, I needn't have worried about outside interference. I put down my bags, stretch my back, and pull open the curtains to reveal a second, thicker set of drapes. The MGM Grand is bathed in green floodlights at night, but there could be a lighthouse outside and the room would remain perfectly black. The dual drapes are a thoughtful touch, really, more elaborate than the mint on the pillow or the sanitary sash on the toilet. I open them. The room fills with daylight.

Time to explore. Tyson won't even be on the casino grounds until late afternoon. His final pre-fight press conference is scheduled for tomorrow morning. I have a good chunk of the day to kill, and I'm running on high. I make the long march to the elevator, plunge down several storeys, thread through the endless rows of slot machines and blackjack tables, locate the hard-to-find exit, and find myself on the strip.

The January sun is shining. The snow may be piling up in Toronto, but in Vegas the temperature is comfortable and the breeze warm. There are few cities in the world, I imagine, with a climate suitable for outdoor escalators. Most of them climb toward pedestrian walkways that arch over the main drag. Such a mechanism connects the MGM Grand to New York, New York — a casino-hotel complex designed to look like Manhattan, complete with a massive replica of the Empire State Building. What the hell,

I think, and start across the bridge. I pause to watch the traffic below until a street vendor selling knockoff Tyson-Botha T-shirts approaches.

"How much?" I ask.

"Five bucks for one, ten for two," he says, taking a couple out of his duffel bag. I thank him for the math lesson and walk toward the roller coaster that threads its way through New York, New York, dipping and twisting between the buildings that make up the imitation skyline. Crowds of people bustle about the sidewalk, many with alcohol in hand. They're wearing golf shirts and white running shoes and jeans with creases. The silhouettes of skyscrapers block out the sky above them. Anywhere else and the sight would have been almost mundane, but here it's exotic. The Chrysler Building in the Nevada desert? Imagine.

To the south beckons the black Pyramid of Cheops and Excalibur, a white castle with red and blue rooftops. But the half-finished Eiffel Tower shimmering to the north catches my eye. Objects here are farther away than they appear, however. Sweat is about to leak through my shirt by the time I reach Paris. It looked to be within easy reach but ends up at least a mile's hike.

The Las Vegas experience overwhelms me en route to a point beyond saturation. The giant Coca-Cola bottle; the monorail; the surf 'n' turf specials and the prime rib; the ever-present ringing of slot machines; the Sphinx; the knights in armour and the Brazilian dancers; the gondolas and the trapeze artists and the indoor fireworks. It's impossible to take in the circus without side effects. Headache. Nausea. Fatigue. A dash of wonder.

The Eiffel Tower, a knockoff like the T-shirts, is spectacular, though not yet complete. Its four legs extend just high enough to meet. Its foundation has been tucked next to a plaster Arc de Triomphe and the grey façade of the Hôtel de Ville. Plywood protects the construction site from vandals and les misérables. Dust blows where there will soon be Louis XIV hedgerows and parking garages.

Las Vegas is in the midst of a revolution. The old casinos are falling at a rapid rate to make room for our postmodern monsters.

Not far from Paris, the Venetian canals have been dug (but are still without water), and a golden Mandalay Bay is about to open its doors close to the airport. Bigger and brighter and built for family fun. Forget about the seedy side of LV, and never mind that slot machines line the shitter at Denny's. Bring the kids and have a ball.

And will it be Tawni, Cheri, or Brandi this evening? The strip is evenly pristine aside from the dead palms and the rows of battered newspaper boxes that clutter the curb. Each box holds an assortment of full-colour hooker catalogues. Johns and conventioneers can pull one out and survey the local girls before making a selection. As advertised, sexual satisfaction arrives at your door after a phone call and the promise of a few Benjamins. One-stop shopping. It all seems very convenient and harmless. But the newspaper boxes are stocked by little Hispanic boys who pedal up and down the strip on rusted bicycles. Instead of baseball cards or sporty decals, baskets full of paper prostitutes hug their rear tires. The kids often stop to offer the catalogues directly to passersby. The elderly men who walk hand in hand with their wives usually decline. But more youthful tourists sometimes take the catalogues and indulge in a quick peek. The dirty books are then dropped to the ground, and alert children can look down at the sidewalk and gain advanced standing in female anatomy. Along the bottom of the plywood fence surrounding Paris, pages upon pages of pink flesh gather like autumn leaves against a barn. Little black boxes cover the eyes of some of the women photographed. Their plastic smiles wear the sheen of crack and crystal meth. I toe the books and scoff at the notion of LV's new reputation as an amusement park.

Something clicks inside me, and I crawl into a dingy holdover from Old Vegas. The air is full of smoke, and the gamblers look to be low-rollers but hardcore. More than a few have no teeth. I'm not much of a gambler, yet, and the veterans intimidate me a bit. I don't really know how to play anything. I decide this isn't a good place to learn the tables, so I pick up a roll of quarters and head for the slots. A mug's game. A sign outside the casino claimed: "Our slots are the loosest." An interesting turn of phrase, I think, as I settle on a machine. The cushion on the adjacent stool has been flattened by a series of wide asses and isn't very comfortable. Good. Won't be here long anyway.

The machine to my left is empty. To my right sits an older man in nylon pants. A cigarette in need of a flick rests between his fingers. He uses the buttons on the slot machine to turn the reels rather than the arm. I decide the old-fashioned way will allow me to nurse my roll. I break it open into one of the plastic cups stacked next to the slots. The coins are greasy. My fingers start to blacken as I feed the change into the maw of my machine. I earn a small return at first, cashing out each time I win and putting the quarters into my cup, just to fool myself that I might leave with a profit. I vow to keep my original investment.

My cup is soon close to empty. My eyes have started to glaze over from the smoke and the lights; the sound of the machines is getting on my wick. Yet I continue to plug in quarters. My hand begins reaching for the black knob at the end of the arm out of instinct. An unfeeling process. Quarter. Pull. Lose. Quarter. Pull. Lose. I feel myself deaden. I wonder if my teeth are growing as loose as the slots.

I leave with four quarters to my name, happy to return to the sunshine. The air is full of car exhaust but seems fresh to my lungs. I point myself toward the MGM Grand, still trying to shake the ringing in my ears.

Nasty business, gambling. Boxing is clean by comparison, and I feel ready for the biggest attraction in Las Vegas. Fuck Wayne Newton. Mike Tyson's back in town.

VICTIMS ALL

The fight between Mike Tyson and François Botha is no morality play, no battle between good and evil. The South African was stripped of his IBF heavyweight crown several months ago when he was caught full of the banned steroid Nandrolone. Botha depended on the dope to speed his recovery from an arm injury, and buckets of it were found in his system. But Botha's trainer, Panama Lewis, had been found guilty of a far greater offence almost two decades earlier. In 1983, he worked with a powerless fighter named Luis Resto. Someone removed the padding from Resto's gloves before his bout against Billy Collins, a young up-and-comer from Tennessee. Collins suffered terrible injuries to his face and was unable to box again. He began to drink heavily and died when he drove his car into a creek nine months after his final fight. As Resto's chief second, Lewis was indictable, and he served almost three years in prison for his crime. He was also banned for life from corners.

Botha's camp applied for the reinstatement of Lewis prior to the fight with Tyson. The request was denied. The irony of the situation — given Tyson's return only nineteen months after biting Holyfield — was not lost on the assembled media pack. But there was little sympathy. Lewis reeked of trouble. His eyes were forever hidden behind dark shades, and he walked like a man who would gladly paralyze another for a bottle of malt. Billy Collins was a popular kid, and boxing writers have long memories. History would never be on Lewis's side.

Such is the strange code that governs boxing. It's still hard for me to understand. Break a man, that's good. Break a rule, that's bad. Except for Mike Tyson. He can fall as far as he likes, because his woe makes for stories that sing. And during the week before his return to boxing, Tyson does not let us down. He is miserable yet fiery, grounded yet on the edge of a cliff. He seems trapped by boxing, and he begins to assume the look of a cornered animal. He talks openly about retirement. Only his financial problems — he owes the IRS about $13 million US — keep him shackled to the sport. He hates the circus. He hates the routine. He hates the press. His eyes sear: "Bring on the noise, motherfuckers . . . You want to see a motherfucking show? . . . I'll stuff everything you need down your motherfucking throats." Yet I can't help laughing the first time I lay eyes on Iron Mike. I expect pure malice, evil incarnate. Instead, his face is coated with make-up.

My first Las Vegas afternoon has disappeared. I return with my dollar to the MGM Grand, revisit my room, pick up my notepad and tape recorder, and head for the fight's expansive media facilities. A huge white tent has been erected behind the hotel. It contains rows of tables and telephones, televisions hooked up to satellites, a stage surrounded by chairs, jugs of drink, and bowls of chips and pretzels. It's designed to make life easier for the writers on deadline. One-stop shopping for whores of a different sort. I show my pass, say hello to a few reporters — some faces are now familiar — and spy Tyson on the stage. He's the most famous individual I've seen in person, an instantly recognizable anti-hero, wearing a smock. A plump, red-haired woman tries to soften his features with powder. She dabs a sponge delicately across his brow, across the expanse of his broad nose and over his pursed mouth. I wonder whether she's nervous. Afterward she says she wasn't. She's applied make-up to a lot of tough guys. Tyson, she says, is a pussycat.

The pussycat is then hooked up to a microphone and propped in front of a television camera. He spends the next hour talking to reporters from around the world, filling two-minute chunks of airtime for the nightly news in Cincinnati and Tampa and London. The reporters in the media tent surround one of the larger televisions, on which each mini-interview is broadcast. Tyson may be nearby in the flesh, but we've all travelled to Las Vegas to watch him on closed-circuit TV. I think back to my interview with Otis Grant and realize that such access will not be the norm. I already miss the intimacy. Michael Katz, his poor-boy cap and neck brace in place, again blocks my view. I can't seem to escape his massive nut. Other reporters crunch on snacks and rattle drinks, laughing and shouting out sarcastic remarks. It's like trying to report on a distant conversation in a subway car crowded with overeaters. I scribble down quotes as best I can, but ascertain only that Tyson is unhappy to lead this pep rally.

He had tried to cloak his bad self over the previous weeks. Under the watchful eye of two public relations consultants, Tyson gave out turkeys at Christmas and talked to juvenile delinquents about his life of crime. But he began to lose his cool as the training became monotonous and the demands more frequent. He bulldogged a television crew out of his Phoenix gym. He erupted during a conference call with reporters when he was asked about his love of Liston. ("I have a great affinity for him," he began; "Motherfuckers," he ended.) And in the middle of this hour-long session under the media spotlight, Tyson again explodes. The make-up woman isn't around to see the display. Otherwise she might have a change of heart.

None of the interviews has gone smoothly. Tyson answers most questions with rolls of his eyes or glib, tired responses. He mocks one reporter by assuming the stance of Uncle Tom — "Yes, massah. No, massah" — and skewers a radio DJ during another interview. Tyson is peppered with the same questions over and over again. Again and again, he responds with taunts and abuse. A television reporter from New York finally brings matters to a head. He pulls the plug on the interview, and Tyson says that's all right with him. The reporter, separated from Tyson by the safety of several thousand miles, throws a verbal jab. Tyson shouts, "Suck off!" in response. The reporters still milling around the television in the media tent joke about the pseudo-slur. Tyson knows he must be a good boy, but he can't quite rein in his rage. Still, in *his* mind he's made a concession. For him, "Suck off!" is an acceptable level of belligerence. We all laugh and record the incident in our notepads, feeling somehow superior, I guess, made holy by distance.

The session ends. Tyson leaves with his entourage, and Botha takes his place. The White Buffalo, as Botha calls himself, looks like a pumped-up Vanilla Ice. His blond hair is tucked under a wide-brimmed hat. He has a matching moustache. He's wearing black pants and a black T-shirt that stretches across his gut. Two pink scars on his elbow provide evidence of his earlier pain, but the needle marks have disappeared.

Unlike Tyson, he chooses not to spar with reporters. He knows how to play the role of supporting actor, and he does his best to win over fight fans. "I believe this is my moment," he says in his thick Afrikaner accent. "This is my dream come true. I've been chasing this goal since I first started in boxing. This is the fight all the heavyweights out there want." A lightweight, Botha adds sternly, he's not. He ends every interview with thanks and a smile. A likeable buckethead.

I fill the evening with a stroll and think about my place in boxing's universe. It won't be as easy as I'd hoped to play kingmaker. As I absorb the energy of the strip, I realize there are hundreds of reporters, with a thousand years of combined service, still huddled in the parking lot of the MGM Grand. It's a sobering thought. There will be no overnight glory. A long road lies ahead. It doesn't disappear in my mind's eye until it reaches a vanishing point a lifetime away. I return to the hotel already feeling outdone. Beaten to the punch.

Before bed I watch the local news, which broadcasts Tyson's interview with the New York reporter. The anchor warns viewers about Tyson's use of profanity before the clip is aired. "Suck" is replaced with a bleep when the tape finally rolls. The implication: Tyson told the reporter to fuck off, which he hadn't. I have no pity for Mike Tyson. He's a bad man and a brute. But as I sit on my king-sized bed in my king-sized room, I decide Tyson has just cause to feel as his psychological tests suggest. The words echo in my head: "used, victimized and treated unfairly." He brings much of the grief upon himself, but the avalanche does not always originate with him. I go to sleep, anger replacing defeat.

The usual suspects gather for the morning's press conference at a double-decker theatre in the MGM Grand. The upper tier is filled with hundreds of fight fans hoping for a glimpse of a sideshow freak. The press occupies the lower level, where a bank of cameras and rows of reporters also await Tyson's arrival. Thankfully, there is more free food. But the clock ticks. The weight of boredom begins to settle on the room. In Chicago, Michael Jordan announces his retirement from basketball. The Windy City is the place to be. We all feel as though we're missing out.

A moment's entertainment is finally provided by Steve (Crocodile) Fitch, Tyson's self-proclaimed master motivator. He is the most recognizable member of Team Tyson, primarily because his booming voice fills the air with annoying regularity, but also because he wears a uniform that consists of wraparound sunglasses, military fatigues, and a matching bandanna. He stomps up and down the aisles of the auditorium. Sweat beads on his forehead. "Guerrilla warfare!" he yells again and again. "He's gonna knock him out! It's guerrilla warfare! Guerrilla warfare!" Two overanxious security guards handcuff the Crocodile and escort him from the theatre. He complains loudly, but he's well accustomed to unwanted attention. He's served time for killing a man. "It was in another life," the Crocodile explains to a reporter. "Guerrilla warfare!" he concludes. The room happily watches the display.

The Crocodile is allowed to return to the theatre after a short detention. He's quick to resume his chant. Reporters wonder whether the incident is a set-up, a feeble attempt to generate excitement for a fight that lacks fizz. The outcome is close to a foregone conclusion despite Tyson's extended absence from the ring; his new camp — including Tommy Brooks, Evander Holyfield's former trainer — is competent but relatively uninteresting; the press has assumed a cynical tone, and the dispatches from Nevada are less than favourable; several thousand tickets are still available, and pay-per-view forecasts are low.

Like the bacon and eggs rumbling in my stomach, all is not sitting right in Vegas. Boxing's safest haven is no longer impressed with boxing's most dangerous man. He's about to be outdrawn by an impressionist named Danny Gans. That's humiliation.

But Tyson continues to tell the city to go suck itself. His promoter, a burly man from Denver named Dan Goossen, belatedly steps up to a podium at centre stage and introduces Tyson and Botha simultaneously. Only the South African, in jeans and a white T-shirt, appears. He enters stage left and assumes his assigned position at a table draped with black cloth. Botha's father, Jan, sits by his side. Tyson is either late or not satisfied with his introduction. The theatre begins to buzz with speculation. Goossen looks toward stage right and nods. He offers a more elaborate introduction, and Tyson emerges from behind the curtain and slowly makes his way to his seat. His sulk continues. He carries himself like a spoiled child on the verge of a tantrum. My early sympathy begins to erode.

Tyson spends much of the press conference with his head on the table in front of him. He refuses to acknowledge the thanks from Botha's camp for the opportunity. Tyson promotes his wife's Be Real line of clothing when it's his turn to speak, but he says nothing of the fight. There are three or four questions from the floor. Tyson offers his most common response to queries. "I don't know anything about that," he repeats. The refrain rivals "Guerrilla warfare!" as the mantra of Tyson's comeback.

But Tyson takes the time to explain his lack of enthusiasm before leaving. "They've put a muzzle on me," he says of his camp. "I really can't express what I really want to say, because I had an incident on television with a gentleman from New York." His handlers didn't appreciate the bad press, whether it was deserved or not. They've clamped down on their difficult client. It's better that Tyson say nothing at all rather than risk further offence. One of the most feared men in the world has been rendered mute by college graduates in suits. It must be difficult for Tyson to submit to their wishes. Or to money's golden handcuffs.

The charismatic Botha takes it all in stride. The press is in turn most grateful for his easy manner and sense of humour. He eats up the attention. His brief hold on the IBF belt notwithstanding, Botha has forever occupied a place on boxing's margins. This is his chance to make a name for himself. After Tyson is ushered through a side exit, Botha takes a chair to the front of the stage and smiles as a media scrum forms below him. His hair has been expertly coiffed. His moustache has been trimmed. His pale blue eyes gleam whenever he flashes a grin. "The man hardly said a word," says

Botha to break the ice. "I think his nerves are killing him. Mike never says a lot. He's never a guy who says much. He lets his fists do the talking, and so do I. But I'm blessed. I can talk."

And talk Botha does. My notepad fills with quote after quote, blue ink that will ultimately become black type. "In the future," he says, "you'll see much more of the White Buffalo. I'm going to be the biggest thing in boxing, because I'm the only white heavy-weight out there that can fight."

"The White Buffalo is a nice guy. He can talk to everybody. He's a family man. He's a regular guy, just like everybody else. I love everybody."

"I'm still young. I'm going to be around a long time. This fight is great publicity for me. Everybody knows now who I am. I'm a young guy. I'm still pretty, and I intend to stay pretty. Come Saturday, that's what I've got to do."

"I'm going to talk to him. I might say things that he won't like, and he might get upset and make a mistake and run into a phantom punch."

"If you look at my body, and the other guys out there . . . who's using steroids, me or they? It set me back tremendously. But now I'm fighting one of the biggest fights in my life."

"I'm not just a tough man who can take a great shot. I've got skills."

"It only takes one punch to rule the whole fight."

"I might bite him first."

The heat of the scrum is overwhelming. My hand begins to cramp from writing quickly. My notepad turns wet in my other fist. One of the reporters pressing against me reeks of white coffee, and his ear boasts a prodigious amount of wax. I'll take a mouthful if he comes any closer. That's it, I've had enough. I want Botha to get up and leave, but he keeps on playing the room. Understandably. His most notable recent bout was a late-round loss to Michael Moorer. Now he has the chance to occupy a part of Mike Tyson's spotlight, and Mike Tyson is only too happy to defer.

★

Another night passes. We gather again at the MGM Grand Theatre for what I've determined is the most pointless exercise in sports: the heavyweight weigh-in. Tyson strips down to a pair of black bikini briefs and steps on the scale. He's one of the world's few short men who can look cut at 223 pounds. Botha, soft and pasty, weighs ten pounds more. The two complete the obligatory staredown. Botha stands perfectly still. Tyson's arms swivel at the shoulder, swinging back and forth like hammers strung up by their handles. He looks ready to pop, but the boxers are quickly separated by their respective camps. Fine theatre.

Greater excitement comes with the unexpected arrival of Muhammad Ali, who testified on behalf of Tyson before the Nevada State Athletic Commission. Ali creeps through the room toward the end of the proceedings. The top of his head pokes up from the middle of a massive throng. A spotlight follows his journey. The crowd begins to chant: "Ali! Ali! Ali!" It's a bittersweet moment that provides an uneasy parallel. Ali was once banished from boxing because he had no quarrel with "them Viet Cong." He returned to the ring in Atlanta in 1970. His first fight was against Jerry Quarry, a white heavyweight with a blond mop, an Irish François Botha. Ali opened a gash above Quarry's left eye and picked at the spot with jab after jab. The referee stopped the fight after three rounds. Ali won the rematch in seven.

Ali looks frail as he climbs the stairs that lead to the stage at the MGM Grand. He now famously battles Parkinson's disease. But his one-time opponent suffered more significant damage. A few days before the Tyson-Botha fight, Jerry Quarry died in a black haze. Quarry first began to exhibit signs of *dementia pugilistica* in 1982. His short-term memory left, his motor skills deteriorated, and his brain was that of a man thirty years his senior. But in 1992, a forty-seven-year-old, barely coherent Quarry found one last fight. He took on a club fighter in Colorado, a state that requires no boxing licence, and was battered for six more rounds. His final fall came six years later, shortly after Christmas. Quarry was survived by his three children, his parents, and Muhammad Ali.

Earlier in the week, Tyson was asked to comment on Quarry's death. "He gave a good contribution to boxing," Tyson replied. "I'm sure he'll be missed. He had a lot of personal problems, and sometimes we become a victim of our personal problems." Another of Tyson's thinly veiled cries for help.

Billy Collins. Muhammad Ali. Jerry Quarry.

Mike Tyson.

THE EAR GUY

Another broken man resides in Las Vegas. His name is Mitch Libonati, a.k.a. the Ear Guy. His name is not instantly familiar, but Mitch knows fame. He found the chunk of Evander Holyfield's ear that Tyson spat out during their second fight. Mitch's claim made him an overnight celebrity, another character in boxing's long drama. I decide he'll make a good story. A sidebar to the Main Event. Mike Tyson's about to return to the ring a few months after his historic act of barbarism. What's happened to the other bit players in the meantime?

I look in the phone book and find a listing for Libonati, M. The guy turns out to be Mitch's brother. Mitch keeps an unlisted number now, but his brother says he'll get us in touch. I wait in my hotel room until the phone finally rings. It's Mitch. He seems timid and shy to talk. He wants to know what I have in mind. I explain that I want to write a story about him. "You know, a 'where are you now' sort of thing," I say.

"Yeah," he replies with a combination of excitement and reservation. "I figured this would happen when Mike came back." He needs significant prodding to come over. I coax and cajole him. He eventually agrees to jump in his car and drive to the MGM Grand. Mitch hasn't returned to the hotel since the night of the bite. "It's been a long time," he says.

There's a knock within minutes. I make sure both sets of drapes are closed and open the door. Mitch stands before me. A stocky guy, his hair has started to thin and he keeps it short. When he smiles his face bunches up in a goofy sort of way, but his eyes are very dark and serious. He's nervous. Guarded even. I extend my hand. He takes one step into the room, stops, and looks around. He listens, too. Part of him thinks our meeting might be a set-up. The hotel hadn't taken kindly to the publicity Mitch received after his gory find. He doesn't want to end up like Liston, sprawled on the floor with a needle in his arm.

Mitch sits down at the table. I pull up a chair. He asks for a cup for the tobacco juice in his mouth. I pass him a glass from the bathroom, but he says he doesn't want to leave a mess for the maid to clean. He picks a paper cup out of the garbage and dispenses with the wad. He then pulls a scrapbook out of a plastic bag and passes it over to me. He starts to tell a story he's told a thousand times.

"That night," he begins, "I was the fifth man in Evander Holyfield's corner." On the first page of the scrapbook is an all-access pass to the fight, dubbed "The Sound and the Fury" by promoter Don King. He held pass No. 2053, valid for one night only. It gleams under the light on the table. "Mitch Libonati, Grand Garden Glovecutter," it reads. The pass gave the twenty-something Mitch the chance to become a star. In the strange way that ordinary people can find fleeting celebrity, his hold on the most gruesome piece of sports memorabilia in history made Mitch Libonati an equally valuable commodity. His pass, too. He says he was offered $3,000 US for the souvenir. He declined the bid.

"Anyway," he says. The night began normally enough for Mitch, who worked at the MGM Grand in the Convention Services division. He helped out with the hundreds of trade shows and concerts that wend their way to Las Vegas. He also helped out whenever the hotel hosted a fight. Mitch was told to stock the locker rooms. He carefully set up massage tables, made certain there was plenty of ice and tape, put up chairs, and laid out bundles of white towels. He didn't know it then, but that night, three hours before the fight, he put out the white towel that would help stop Holyfield's bleeding. "The most fascinating things go on in the locker rooms," says Mitch. "There's no better feeling than fight night."

Mitch next made his way to the ring. He wanted to be sure everything was in place. Minutes later he stood alone on the canvas during the quiet before the boxing storm. He enjoyed a prophetic daydream. "I remember just standing in the middle of the ring, looking around thinking to myself, 'Someday you'll make a name in the sport.' Every fight, I always said that to myself. I thought I'd be a great manager or someone who bettered boxing. To have it happen finding a piece of ear. . . ." He tries to focus on something beyond the ceiling. "It's kind of funny," he finally continues.

Mitch was perched ringside throughout the match. It was his job to dry the mat and clean up the blood after the fight. He had stored pathology bags under the ring. Some of them were already filled with the stained wraps of the undercard, and he had put on a fresh pair of latex gloves. The third round came. Mitch heard a woman scream, "He bit him!" He looked up and watched as Tyson dispensed with the chunk of ear. At first he thought it was a mouthguard. "But then I put the two together," says Mitch, the thrill building in his voice. "He bit and spit. There was a piece of Evander."

The fight continued. The ear somehow stuck to the canvas. Tyson bit Holyfield a second time, and Holyfield jumped around the ring wildly. Still, the ear remained where it had landed. Mitch kept his eye on the chunk when Mills Lane ended the fight. The corners filled the ring. Police officers and security guards jumped through the ropes. Mitch piled in with them. He has watched the fight film a hundred times now. He always freezes at the moment when Mitch Libonati, about to become forever known as the Ear Guy, appears next to Holyfield in the confusion. A few seconds of mayhem passed. Mitch looked at his feet. He saw the ear up close — "It looked like a piece of sausage," he says — picked it up, and changed his humble life.

He grabbed a spare latex glove out of his back pocket. He put the chunk of ear into it and asked a security guard to escort him to the dressing room. Mitch talked to one of the boxer's handlers: "I have something of Evander's," he said three times. He tried to stay calm, but his heart was pumping hard. The handler didn't believe him. Mitch held up the glove as proof of his find. But the chunk had slipped into the glove's index finger, and for a heart-stopping moment Mitch thought he'd lost it. It was the handler, his eyes wide, who spotted the sacred tissue. He grabbed the glove out of Mitch's hands and disappeared into the locker room. That, Mitch says, was the last time he saw his trophy.

What happened next to the ear is unknown. The *New York Post* reported that the chunk was reattached successfully, but the story turned out to be false. There were also reports that the ear was lost on the way to the hospital, that a hotel security guard stole it, that an ambulance attendant had decided to pocket a piece of boxing history. A New York commodities trader said he had bought the ear for $18,000 US. A collector in Philadelphia also claimed ownership and offered the ear on the open market for $30,000 US.

Mitch says he often worries that people might try to fake his find. "Maybe somebody went to a friend's house and bit somebody's ear, and now they say they have Holyfield's ear," he says. I smile. "You might laugh," he continues, "but you think how crazy this world is. Billy Bob might bite Jimmy's ear, and say, 'Hey, I've got Evander Holyfield's ear.' It's sick." But Mitch pauses to consider how much the ear might have been worth, especially after Mark McGwire's seventieth home-run ball sold at auction for $3 million US. "Seriously, after the McGwire thing, I thought about it," he admits. "I probably could have sold it to somebody, some wacko. I found a piece of ear. It's better than catching a ball. There's a difference. I mean, a body part? Come on."

I laugh quietly. The whole story seems unique to boxing's ugly spectacle. A bizarre piece of Americana. But Mitch takes his fate seriously; he becomes very quiet when he tells me what happened after he found the ear. He was guided to his car, past the first wave of the media barrage. He drove to his mom's house. The phone began to ring at five o'clock in the morning: "Next thing you know," he says, "microphones, cameras, boom. Stories, boom. Reporters were all over. It didn't stop. Story after story, interview after interview." I flip through the scrapbook as he spins his tale. On a yellow sheet of paper there's a list of the television and radio stations and newspapers that filled his answering machine with messages. He was on morning shows across the country. He was in *Sports Illustrated* and *The Ring* magazine. He was on CNN and *Entertainment Tonight*. Even David Letterman welcomed him onstage, where he sat next to actor Tom Arnold.

"It was awesome, just awesome," he says with a rare smile. But then he turns bitter with regret. "I got a lot of attention," he says. "But I think I blew it. I really do. I wish I would have run with it. I would do it again, but I would do it a whole lot different. I would go with every opportunity I could." Aside from a year-long car lease offered by Saturn in exchange for wearing a company shirt on Letterman, Libonati didn't profit from his sudden fame. Maybe, he now thinks, he should have taken one of the book deals he was offered — "For thin ones," he says — or made a few commercials. He tried to make it as a boxing manager and trainer, but he wasn't able to break into the business. And he couldn't bring himself to set up tables for hardware shows. He quit his job without ever returning to the hotel. Not until tonight, some nineteen months later.

"I think after all the TV and radio shows, I just freaked a little," he says. "Since the Bite Night, I stayed away from boxing. I just didn't want to deal with any more fights. Now, it eats at me. I miss it. There will never be anything better for me. It was the most exciting night of my life, and it will never be erased. I'm a trivia answer. I'm a tiny part of history."

Mitch now works construction. He digs suburban pools and paves suburban driveways. Nobody recognizes him. "After all that," he says, "I'm driving a tractor. I swear, I could be up on the mountains working, and I just find myself staring at the hotel, thinking about it. I did something incredible, and then I bailed. It's tough. It was the most important thing I've ever done."

He readies himself to leave. It's after midnight.

"You want an autograph?" he asks. I guess he hasn't been asked for it lately, and I humour him. Mitch signs my notebook the way he always signs his name now. He writes "the Ear Guy" after his signature and accents it with a tiny rendering of an ear in quick, practised strokes.

"Hey, send me the article so I can add it to the scrapbook."

I tell him I will.

He shakes my hand and walks toward the door, stops and turns around. "Can you do me a favour?" he asks. "If anyone wants to do something with the Ear Guy, tell them to call me. I'm in Vegas and I'm undecided." I say okay. He steps into the hallway, looks both ways first, as though crossing a street, and the door closes quietly behind him.

THE SOUND OF TANKS

There is no official business scheduled for Saturday morning. The calm of the dawn. I decide to set the scene for the fight by watching the strippers and high-rollers practise their dances on strangers and craps tables. I hike to the elevators and cautiously press one of the brass buttons. After spending only a few minutes in this place, a man carries enough energy to transmit blue sparks between hand and metal. Every ungrounded step risks the sensation of chewing tinfoil. The elevator doors open. A man with a Tyson-Botha cap laughs as he watches me select a floor with great care. "My wife refuses to touch anything in this place," he says with a southern drawl. "She's been shocked too many times." Fortunately for Tyson, boxing fans aren't so quick to become shy.

The doors open to a crowded casino floor. It's pure Scorsese. Everything seems to move in slow motion. Hard music plays inside my head. Men in sharp suits and women in tight dresses roar and throw dice and drop chips. The air is filled with the smoke of a million cigars — none of them Cuban. Every sense is pounded into submission. It's easy to feel drunk in Vegas without taking a drop.

The rooms begin to spin all on their own.

I head for the box office to see if any seats are still available for the fight. There are plenty. But a long line has formed outside the ticket booths. Real people have decided to show at the last possible minute. The house will still be papered with hotel employees, and 8,000 seats have been picked up by other casinos as gifts for their favourite customers. Regardless, more than 14,000 people will await Tyson tonight. And judging from the brisk sales at a Tyson souvenir stand nearby, where leather jackets are going for 300 bills and T-shirts for two dimes, most of the crowd will be in his corner.

The more upscale clothiers inside the MGM Grand are also doing well. I'm noticing that fights are notorious vehicles for the fuzzy-dice set. They want to look their tacky best. But sharkskin doesn't come cheap. I'm drawn to a particular boutique because of the remarkable number of orange suits on display. Inside, rack after rack of tailored fabric matches the city's neon fireworks. Nothing so plain as black or white. Bright and bold. Flash and dash. These people are spending serious green to look like Flintstones vitamins. A man stands next to the counter with a bagged Zegna suit. I ask the manager how much the guy paid for it. "Oh," he smirks, "a few thousand dollars." How many thousands? Another smirk. "Eight," he says.

There's another excited bunch in Las Vegas. The cops are on edge, trigger-happy and prepared for the worst. Brownshirts are everywhere. An unsavoury crowd clings to boxing. The last time Tyson was in town, guns were flashed on the casino floor and bullets tore through the felt on the blackjack tables. The MGM Grand was shut down for hours after the fight, long enough to dent the casino's earnings for that quarter. But baccarat drop, a sign of high-roller activity, skyrocketed during fight week. Fans arrived for the show but also wanted to put on their own. Sometimes that meant the law got broken, and the cops knew only too well what drink and gambling and bravado can combine to make. I ask one officer what to expect. "It will be a melee," he says. "Things happen in Las Vegas that don't happen anywhere else." He asks me where I'm from. "Canada," I say. "Take care of yourself," he replies.

The metal detectors work overtime at the airport, where fight fans and celebrity seekers are being dumped by the planeload. Shortly after lunch, taxis and limousines begin to pour onto the strip. An army of hookers from across the southwest has descended on the major casinos. Pimps supervising their migration smoke next to banks of slot machines. Other tough characters loiter in dark corners. Several handshakes involve money and plastic bags. Everyone wears masks that say, "Don't fuck with me." Fired-up men take no notice. Fights break out between groups of Tyson supporters. Even the weather turns ugly. Black clouds crowd out the blue skies.

The afternoon fast becomes memory. It's four o'clock when I pull on my decidedly drab suit, find my seat at the MGM Grand Garden Arena, and await Tyson's return.

Jack Nicholson, Pamela Anderson, Bruce Willis, Mariah Carey, Linda Evangelista, Donald Trump, Matt Damon, and a hundred other stars join me over the next few hours. Alcohol flows freely. Gang members stake out their positions. There must be a thousand bodyguards in here.

The undercard is grim but violent, a parade of no-hopers ducking punches and fate. Music pounds out of loudspeakers when men don't pound on each other. The crowd has been topped up with fuel to burn. Roads to drive. I feel my body enter fight mode. My stomach begins to kick. The reporters on either side of me are from France and Japan; they look aghast, as though they're witnessing hate crimes. They ain't seen nothing yet, I tell myself, feeling like a veteran.

Eyelids don't work as well as usual, jammed open by fever. We stare at giant television screens suspended from each corner of the arena. They relay an image of the door to François Botha's locker room. The door opens. The crowd roars.

My movements become automatic.

★

Botha, surrounded by his entourage, enters to the music of Journey. The song about heart. He knows he'll need to swallow hard. A South African flag flutters above him. His father walks behind him, holding his son's shoulders as the Botha camp cuts through the crowd. Botha himself wears black trunks and a massive white animal skin as a cape. Probably fake. He looks afraid at first, but then the adrenaline begins to flow. His eyes grow hard as he reaches the ring. He climbs through the ropes and starts to dance. He ditches the cape. Punches the air. Steals energy from the crowd.

More ominous music fills the air. The fans take to their feet. A gangsta rap track slams into high gear. Cameras follow Tyson as he leaves his locker room and marches down the concourse toward the main arena. He's surrounded by massive black men in white suits. The spotlights converge on an opening in the crowd. Team Tyson appears. The arena shakes with the sound of tanks, but heartbeats can be heard above the noise. Ears begin to bleed. Glasses threaten to shatter. Botha flips a switch and goes haywire. He bounces around the ring, yelling to himself and to the crowd. He stares at Tyson, but Tyson pays no mind. He's in another place. His feet begin to tense in black boots. His black trunks shine with perspiration. The wait is almost over. He ducks through the ropes and paces. Botha calls him on. He uses racial taunts to try to make Tyson snap with fury. Tyson continues to ignore him. Botha is undeterred. He steps up his verbal assault throughout the introductions. A hundred jackhammers fire up when the announcer points to Tyson. He raises his arms to reveal the tattoo of Che Guevera that covers his stomach. Che's face distorts as Tyson twists his body in preparation. There is fire inside him.

Richard Steele, the veteran referee charged with a most unenviable task, calls the two men to the centre of the ring. The corners evacuate the canvas. An electrical charge sweeps through the arena. The opening bell rings.

Botha fights to survive. His strategy works. He clinches Tyson repeatedly. Six, seven, eight times. He then pushes Tyson off and throws a combination.

Tyson begins to anger. He's frustrated by the South African's tactics. At the same time, Botha talks to Tyson. "Come on!" Botha yells. "Is that all you've got?" Tyson forgets to box. He swings one wild punch at a time. Suddenly he's on a Brooklyn street.

Botha steps out of the way easily and counters. He cuts Tyson above the right eye, as Holyfield did nineteen months ago. Tyson panics. At the end of the round everything falls apart.

The two men are tied together when the bell rings. Tyson won't let go. He twists Botha's arm at the elbow and tries to break it. Botha looks up at the bright lights that hang from the ceiling and howls in pain. His white mouthguard almost falls out.

Tyson continues to bend Botha's arm. Botha throws a punch. Then another. Tyson returns the punches.

The corners leap into the ring. Two dozen police officers and hotel security guards follow. Somewhere, Mitch Libonati wishes he was ringside. Tyson and Botha continue to brawl. The crowd holds its breath. It's mayhem in Las Vegas.

The round-card girl jumps gamely to the ropes. She nearly takes an elbow to the face and is pulled to safety. No round-card girl? I'm told that's the equivalent of boxing Armageddon.

The arena rocks with rage. White fans start to look for the exits. White reporters begin folding up their computers and packing their bags. The French guy next to me looks as though he's wet his pants. Mean things happen when fights end badly. California rapper Tupac Shakur was shot to death after Tyson pummelled Bruce Seldon in 1996. How many guns are unholstered this second? How many bullets itch to fly?

Finally, thankfully, order is restored. The crowd offers huge applause. Both fighters have been warned. The fight itself will go on. Lost in the chaos was one hard fact: Botha won the round.

Tyson begins the second round with three quick lefts. None connects. He holds Botha and throws an elbow. Botha and Tyson both complain to the referee. Steele takes a point away from Tyson. Botha clinches again. Tyson uses a right hand to break free. He throws another right hand. Botha counters.

★ ★ ★ IN HIS FIRST FIGHT SINCE BITING EVANDER HOLYFIELD'S EAR, MIKE TYSON TRIES TO BREAK FRANÇOIS BOTHA'S ARM

Botha now taunts Tyson without restraint. He drops his hands. He stands perfectly still and asks for a punch. He sticks out his chin in defiance. Tyson looks silly when he attempts to connect with a haymaker. The round ends with an exchange of late punches.

Botha wins the round.

The pattern continues in the third: Botha clinches, punches, mocks. Tyson slows down. He begins to stiffen with ring rust. Botha somehow boxes Tyson's ears with a simultaneous left and right. A telling moment about a fight and a career.

Botha wins the round.

The fourth begins. Botha lands a solid combination. Tyson responds with a left that stuns his opponent. Botha is cut on the bridge of his nose. His right eye swells. He presses forward. Botha clinches and exits with a combination.

Tyson looks to Steele as though asking for help. He doesn't want to break again. He doesn't want to snap. "C'mon!" Tyson pleads to no avail. Botha laughs. "You're losing, Mike!" he yells. "I'm beating you!"

The evidence backs Botha's case. He wins another round.

The bell rings. The fifth round starts.

Tyson senses defeat. He fights hard. He lands a left that sends a shower of sweat from Botha's head. Another left lands. Tyson connects with yet another left to Botha's mouth. Botha responds with a couple of shots.

Then comes The Punch. Seconds remain in the round when the balls of Tyson's feet first grip the canvas. His calves and thighs twist in unison. His hips swing back and to the left as his right arm uncoils. The muscles of his back make like a football team's offensive line. His fist drives forward and connects with Botha's jaw. Botha's head snaps back. His eyes close.

Botha falls to his knees and then forward. He lifts his head up and lurches to his left and then to his right. He staggers to his feet but tips over backward. Only the ropes keep him in the ring. He soon finds himself in the same position as hundreds of vanquished heavyweights before him. He sees nothing but black when he lands on his back. Tyson is declared the winner. Botha was right when he said one punch would rule the whole fight. But he hadn't planned on taking it.

It's something to see, a man being put down. A snuff movie in the flesh. At that instant, the point of this entire exercise is brought home to me. My job is to report on the arrival of another man's coma, to detail its heavy descent. "This, dear readers, is how it went down, how Botha came to blow his teeth out his nose." I can't deny how awful it all is. Or how mesmerizing. Botha's loss of balance represents our departure from the everyday. Even in Las Vegas, pain is not mainstream. We're here to escape civilization. This fight has given us freedom.

The crowd roars its approval.

Tyson checks on Botha as he comes around. Iron Mike receives congratulations from his camp. The Crocodile struts across the ring. "Guerrilla warfare!" he bellows above the din. Reporters rush to the media tent for the post-fight press conference. But Tyson stays in the ring to meet the demands of television. He pulls on a black skullcap and accepts the microphone.

"I'm not afraid of dying," he says suddenly. He wipes his face with his hands. Wet wraps are still taped to his knuckles. "When I die, I'm going to paradise," he continues. "I'm in a hurry to die."

Tyson's words linger above the ring, above the fight's clutter. I wonder why his claim sounds so familiar. Then I remember Sonny Liston. And I remember that Paradise is just a fancy name for a place by the airport.

WINS AND LOSSES

Mike Tyson sits close to François Botha on the stage in the hot and crowded media tent. Security is not especially tight, and dozens of fans and bangers have made their way inside. Tempers flare and scraps break out intermittently. It's difficult to hear the questions, but the answers make clear the feelings of the fighters: Botha is disappointed and Tyson is relieved.

"I was really controlling it really easily," says Botha. His fog has lifted, but his nose and eye are red and swollen. "I let my guard down. I started fooling around too much. I just walked into the punch and Mike has got a lot of power. A punch that I didn't see."

"I didn't even know I threw it," responds Tyson. "I just saw him on the floor. I thought he was quitting." Tyson laughs, and the fans in attendance laugh with him. Yet there remains something uncomfortable about the affair. The former heavyweight champion of the world is lucky to leave with a victory. The layoff cost him dearly. He's a fighter in decline and a boxer of fading confidence. A man only slightly more skilled than Botha — or Botha himself, had he kept his head — could have made it three defeats in a row for Tyson, two at the hands of Evander Holyfield and one at the hands of some pug. What then? Where could he go from there?

But a single punch finds its mark, and Tyson is vindicated and left unconcerned. He's in the mood to celebrate. Conveniently, Muhammad Ali is celebrating his fifty-seventh birthday the next day. A lavish party, where Tyson appears, is thrown at the MGM Grand. Reporters are welcome.

Earlier in the week, I ran into Ali, his wife, and an assistant in an elevator. The doors opened, and one of history's strongest men stood before me. Shocked, I opened my mouth but made no sound. Ali turned away from me, his feet shuffling in tiny circular steps. He turned back around and held out a brochure that celebrated Allah. He pressed the green paper into my hand. It was autographed. I smiled and said, "Thank you, champ." I stepped out of the way. He left the elevator. A massive mob formed around him within seconds. I watched the fray for a short while, entered the elevator, hit the button for my floor, received a healthy shock, went back to my room, and put the brochure inside a book for safekeeping.

And tonight it's his birthday party. What the hell do you get Muhammad Ali?

A hotel ballroom plays host. The walls are decorated with portraits of Ali as a young man. A table in one corner of the room bears a white cake in the shape of a boxing ring, complete with a set of chocolate boxing gloves. The cake reads, "57 and still The Greatest." A velvet rope separates the table from the press. Reporters and cameramen and photographers gather on one side; official guests and Ali's family stand on the other. Ali is greeted with a rousing cheer when he arrives, and the mask he now wears over his face becomes less stiff. He makes his way to the cake, surrounded by a crowd of well-wishers. The cameramen and photographers strain to get the shot. One photographer scrambles over the rope. Then another. A third man, with a camera on his shoulder, also tries to jump across the divide, but he hooks his foot on the rope and falls to the floor. The barricade collapses with him, and the media rushes toward Ali.

Mass confusion mars the evening. Concerned guests make like riot police and push back the throng. Ali's wife seems frightened and holds her husband at the elbow. He looks as though the slightest push or shove will drop him to the floor. My lungs empty with worry until the commotion fortunately subsides. Ali finally gets to eat a piece of his cake, playfully smearing vanilla icing across his face. He casts his wide eyes toward me. "Happy Birthday, champ," I say. Even though he can't hear me, I'm sure he feels the reverence. My present to him.

Tyson stands next to Ali. He's wearing a suit and is looking positively urbane. He's gentle and generous with his mentor, holding Ali by the arm and guiding him to the children in the room. The kids rally around the two men and bathe them with giggles and joyous shouts. Tyson smiles, seemingly for the first time in weeks. Ali, too, looks happy. The scene is a much-needed antidote to a tough spell. Love has replaced hate.

CP PICTURE ARCHIVE (Nick Ut)

★ MUHAMMAD ALI
THE NIGHT BEFORE HIS FIFTY-SEVENTH BIRTHDAY ★★★

THROW AWAY THE KEY

Desert reservoir blue passes below me once again. I read bits of Mailer and David Remnick's article in an old *New Yorker* on Tyson's second collapse against Holyfield. It's called "Kid Dynamite Blows Up." A fantastic story, as removed from my weekend's harried work as the plane is from the desert. Remnick gets inside Tyson more cleanly than any boxer ever could. It reads like biography. I try to drum out the rhythm and commit it to memory like a song lyric.

I'll need no such device to take Vegas home. Some kind of trip. An eye opener, like a morning cocktail. I carry a strange combination of arrival and fear of never making it, the deflation of my in-check ego. Remnick's superiority again puts me in my place, which I now know to be one seat among hundreds. I am a drop in the spit bucket.

Despite the blow, however, I feel an intense connection with boxing. I thought it would take more time to develop, but our bond drifts nearly as deep as the snow at home. I feel passion for the game, longing when I'm away from it. I walk to the corner store, and I imagine a boxer doing his roadwork. Heat pours out of the vents in my apartment's floor, and I'm transported to a hot gym. I go to sleep and dream about fights. I wake up half-expecting my eyes to be swollen shut.

But they are always open for postcards from my new fixation. Word arrives not long before Valentine's Day that Tyson has been sentenced to serve yet another year in prison. He punched a fifty-two-year-old man in the jaw and kicked a sixty-year-old man in the groin after a minor traffic accident in Maryland. The charges weighed him down prior to his fight with Botha. The conviction will send him to the canvas. His body will fail along with his temper. He'll emerge from jail fat and distracted. The Nevada State Athletic Commission will tell him to find a new home. Sin City is for families now, not for the likes of Iron Mike. I'm grateful that I had the chance to see him before he disappears from view. A chance to see the man before he dissolves into myth.

After his fight with Botha, Tyson said: "It's only a matter of time." He meant that he was close to his old form. But he could have been talking about his sentence. He will now pace inside a different sort of cell, far removed from the confines of the ring.

★ **3** ★

GOING THE DISTANCE FROM REALITY

★ TREVOR BERBICK V. SHANE SUTCLIFFE ★

FEBRUARY 5, 1999

I find I am excited, so excited that I can hardly hold the pencil in my trembling hand. I think it is the excitement that only a free man can feel, a free man starting a long journey whose conclusion is uncertain.

— STEPHEN KING, *RITA HAYWORTH AND SHAWSHANK REDEMPTION*

LARRY HOLMES RUINED MY LIFE

It's February and I'm in Montreal when Mike Tyson is sentenced to his year in prison for assault. I'm here to see Trevor Berbick, the man Tyson defeated in 1986 to claim his first heavyweight title. Berbick held the title for only eight months, but he still believes he's the champion of the world. True enough, he's about to challenge a bruising twenty-three-year-old named Shane Sutcliffe for the Canadian heavyweight crown. But that's where his sense of triumph should end. Berbick claims to be only forty-four years old. He's actually closer to forty-seven, possibly forty-eight. He's also fat, insolvent, and unwell in the deepest sense.

Before I meet Berbick, I dig through years of newspaper clippings and fight reports. It's futile to try to piece together his story. Though I find fragments of his life's narrative, there are holes in the plot that even Berbick is unable to fill. Fight records prove that he's enjoyed moments of glory. He beat John Tate, Pinklon Thomas, and Muhammad Ali in The Greatest's last fight. Different records confirm defeats — at the hands of Tyson, journeymen, street toughs, and sheriffs from upstate New York and Miami. He's also lost twice to the legendary Larry Holmes. They fought once in the ring. Holmes then became Berbick's arch-enemy and later took care of business in a hotel parking lot. The unsanctioned bout made news across North America. It was one of Berbick's last front-page appearances.

Berbick soon dropped out of sight. He was lonely and forgotten. He served time in prison, lived in seedy motels, fought bush-league fights, and did laundry only when he could spare the quarters. Boxing had made Trevor Berbick. It then snapped him in two. That part of his story can be told with singular conviction.

I spoke with Tom McCluskey, Berbick's first professional trainer, before making the trip to Montreal. I knew Berbick was prone to invention and exaggeration, and I wanted an independent voice of reason in the story I was about to spin.

McCluskey met Berbick at an international tournament in 1975. The following year, after Berbick competed for Jamaica at the Montreal Olympics, he adopted Halifax as his hometown and McCluskey as his chief second. McCluskey has since escaped from boxing. He lives in Dartmouth, Nova Scotia, and makes chicken-wing sauce for local restaurants. But even he thinks about what might have been. "Trevor's a very sad story, if you want to dig into the dark side of things," McCluskey told me, his voice pure East Coast. "But I'm not going to do that, because I'm not going to be around much longer. Life is too short, right? But the heavyweight title meant nothing. What good is it if you don't have good people around you, if people don't look up to you? We could have had a good thing. He could have been king of the walk. But you fall and people want to get away from you as quick as they can. There's no in-between.

"But I'm not throwing rocks at anybody," McCluskey concluded. "I wish him all the best. And I hope God blesses him along the way."

Berbick believes he has already.

The weigh-in is the day before the fight at a dumpy hotel close to Olympic Stadium. I suppose we're in a ballroom. The walls are coated with pink stucco, the foam ceiling is stained with patches of brown, and the vinyl chairs are worn thin after a thousand budget weddings. Montreal's considerable boxing community barks out greetings in English and French and a combination of the two. Shane Sutcliffe, a lumberjack of a man from British Columbia, is there with his handlers. He looks thick in every sense of the word and is a lock to win. He's in line to fight John Ruiz on the undercard of the upcoming bout between Evander Holyfield and Lennox Lewis in

New York. He's looking forward to a taste of metropolitan success.

Sutcliffe's more immediate opponent has yet to appear. I'm not surprised. Berbick doesn't relish the prospect of standing on a scale. It's perhaps his worst enemy after Larry Holmes. It will tell him exactly how far he's fallen, and he doesn't need his woes quantified. Wet from the hard rain falling outside, he eventually rolls into the room, stepping gently despite his massive frame. He laughs and jokes with strangers as he makes his way through the tidy bunch of interested parties. He holds up his arms in mock victory. He's transported to a happier time.

Berbick is asked to strip down. He takes off a pair of overalls, a sweater, and a jacket to reveal a singlet and long underwear tucked into wool socks. He looks like a rodeo clown, but he refuses to take off the undergarments before he confronts the scale. The beast reads 247 pounds. Even Berbick looks shocked. His ideal fighting weight was 218 pounds. "Tomorrow I'll be 240," he shouts to the reporters present, many of whom laugh. "You watch," he says earnestly. "I just ate." Berbick dresses and consents to a media scrum. His eyes are bright and happy for the attention, but there's an acute sense of vacancy.

Berbick states, as though fiction were fact, that he'll soon fight for the world title. He's no longer a ranked fighter, but he's convinced he's Contender No. 1. The reporters provide encouragement and smile in response to the boasts. Berbick absorbs the warmth. He begins speaking more rapidly. The words pour out with failing form. He slurs a bundle of unrelated thoughts into a single rant, and he crosses the line that divides curiosity from freak. As he rambles about his devotion to God and herbalism and his soul, the microphones are pulled away and the tape recorders turned off. The reporters slowly begin to disappear, leaving the show early like disgusted movie-goers. "There is a spirit in this title, maybe it is God, but there is a spirit in this Canadian affair that will move me to rise like an eagle," Berbick tells his thinning audience. "I will move mountains. I am preserved. I am a miracle." It seems that few will witness it.

As the proceedings wind down — Sutcliffe is found to carry 233.6 chiselled pounds — Berbick scans the depleted crowd for welcoming ears. I offer mine. We adjourn to an empty meeting room. Berbick's brother Fred, his lone handler, joins us. He sits in silence at one end of a long table, Trevor Berbick at the other. I sit next to him. I put my tape recorder on the table and press Record. Berbick sees the red light go on. I ask him three questions. He speaks for an hour. I've come to understand there are few athletes more press-friendly than former champions: every interview represents one more chance to be remembered.

"I think I can fill you in," he says dreamily, a smile dimpling his round face. "I can tell you about my life." He gets comfortable, taking off his jacket. Across its back in red script is stitched "Trevor Berbick. WBC World Heavyweight Champion." Berbick has worn the jacket since 1986, his halcyon days.

"I won eleven professional fights to start my career," he begins. I glance at the fight records in my hand. They confirm the claim. Berbick was relatively powerless as an Olympian, but Tom McCluskey transformed him into a defensive specialist. The strategy was unspectacular but fail-safe. Berbick often went the distance, but he always came out on top. Word spread about the talented up-and-comer. Berbick's reputation reached the great Archie Moore in California. He smelled cash and convinced Berbick to split with McCluskey. Moore tried to make Berbick more aggressive in the ring, but the hard-charging style was an ill fit. Berbick went down to an early defeat, sidetracked by a legend, and begged McCluskey to return to his side.

In 1980, Berbick landed his first big fight. He was to meet John Tate, the former WBA champion, on the undercard of "The Brawl in Montreal." The night's climax was a hugely hyped battle between Sugar Ray Leonard and Roberto Duran, presented by Don King. (The same fight immortalized on the wall of Dewith Frazer's club outside Toronto.) Berbick fell behind early when it was his time to shine, but he came back to stop Tate in the ninth round. He was suddenly on the fast track to fame. Don King, ever the shock-haired huckster, stopped by Berbick's dressing room and talked to the then lean fighter late into the night. King guaranteed Berbick a title shot should he join the promoter's stable. But King never makes a promise without strings attached — to purses in particular. "The Tate fight opened the door wide," McCluskey told me from Dartmouth. "I knew Trevor wouldn't stay with us. I'm not a genius, but I knew it was time to get out. I know how Don King operates. That's too big-time for me."

The same was likely true for Berbick, who, to be mild, is not well regarded for his intelligence or business acumen. He picked up his title shot, however, against Larry Holmes in 1981. Not yet sworn enemies, the pair met in Nevada to determine the WBC heavyweight champion. Berbick was the first man to go the distance against Holmes in a championship fight, but he found himself on the losing end of a decision. The loss — and the spectre of the victorious Holmes — continues to haunt him.

Berbick dissolves into a furious frenzy when I ask about the fight, touching a nerve that pains him like ringing in his ears. To be honest, I'm afraid. His eyes grow dark and his lips peel back. Spit flies from his mouth and his fists clench tightly. Berbick could choke a man like me to death with relative ease. With only his pint-sized brother within earshot, I imagine myself taking my last breath as Berbick bawls, "Larry Holmes ruined my life! Larry Holmes ruined my life!"

Berbick takes to his feet. He punches the air. "I was going to knock him out!" he cries. "I was going to knock him out with a left hook!" — if only the timekeeper hadn't rung the bell early to end the seventh round, unjustly wresting the championship from his clutches. The Early Bell is one of many conspiracies to which Berbick currently subscribes. They relieve failure's strain. But now he's on the verge of tears. He bangs the table with his fist. It sounds like a cannon going off. "That's why Larry Holmes never fought me again!" he rages. "He knew I could knock him out! He was saved by the bell! He was saved by the bell!" Berbick is alight. I grimace and await my demise. But Berbick suddenly runs into a wall.

He stops cold, returns to his chair, and takes a few deliberate breaths. "I could have beat him," he says quietly. He searches my eyes for traces of belief. "But I was denied," Berbick insists in resignation's whisper. "I was denied." The room is silent for a beat or two. A smile returns to his face. We're friends again. My body slumps in relief as we continue to talk, but I'm still on edge, fearing another outburst.

Shortly after the Holmes fiasco, Berbick accepted the fight against Muhammad Ali. It would be Ali's last appearance in the ring. McCluskey, who had stayed in touch with Berbick, counselled against the fight. Ali had held on too long. But Ali called Berbick's house personally and convinced the youngster to accept the hollow challenge. It was a shameful event. The pair met on December 11, 1981, in a makeshift stadium in the Bahamas, because no American venue would play host. To underscore the embarrassment, someone realized there wasn't a bell at ringside shortly before the fight. A labourer was forced to wander into a nearby pasture and steal one from the neck of an obliging cow. Berbick then took the decision from an uninterested Ali. Both men were hurt by the mismatch, and each would soon find himself absent from the spotlight. Berbick fought infrequently afterward. Only minor titles — the Canadian heavyweight title, the British Commonwealth championship, and the U.S. Boxing Association belt — came his way. His name was more often in the news for his exploits outside the ropes.

In 1986, Berbick was stripped of his Canadian title on the grounds of inactivity. He refused to return the belt and was sued by the Canadian Professional Boxing Federation for $1,500. Berbick claims the incident was a media fabrication. He says he gave up the title voluntarily, and the lawsuit was manufactured by unnamed enemies. Perhaps Larry Holmes had something to do with it. Hell, Holmes owns most of Easton, Pennsylvania. Why not the Canadian justice system, too?

But Berbick recovered to earn a second title shot, two months after his run-in with Canadian boxing authorities and five years after his first bid for the championship. He was pitted against the undefeated Pinklon Thomas, who had inherited the WBC belt from Holmes. Berbick entered the Las Vegas ring a 6–1 underdog. He was supposed to be a roll-over. But he won a twelve-round decision. Only 2,000 spectators watched the fight, and Berbick took home only $50,000 US, but overnight he had become the world's best.

Mike Tyson put an end to Berbick's reign eight months later. Consequently, Mike Tyson, Don King, and Hall of Fame trainer Angelo Dundee became entangled in Berbick's complex web of conspiracies. He was confident going into the ring with Tyson. "He has a big, fat head," Berbick joked before the fight. "I like that. He can't hide a big, fat head." But Berbick's own head had begun to play tricks on him. He spent eight days in hospital before the fight. Tom McCluskey won't tell me why exactly. "His thinking material wasn't clear at that time," he says. "That's as easy as I can put it."

I ask Berbick about his stay at the hospital. He says Don King poisoned him. He also says some sort of gas was pumped into his hotel room through the air-conditioning system. He claims Dundee, who trained Berbick only for the Tyson fight, was out to "hypnotize" him. He also says he was given a mysterious injection before the fight. The world saw Berbick hit the canvas at 2:35 of the second round, the victim of a right hand to the kidney and a left to the head. What the world did not see, Berbick insists, was the poison that would not allow him to stand. "I was denied my goal deliberately. Don King told me straight up: I had to give the belt up because they wanted a young, American challenger to win the championship," he says passionately. "I wanted to keep the title for a long time, but it wasn't my choice. I had to go along with the game." Or what? "Otherwise," says Berbick, his story held together by still more fiction, "I would have had an accident in the desert."

I wouldn't put anything past boxing, even this early into my career, and part of me wants to believe Berbick. There's something childlike about him that tugs at my heartstrings. He has few men in his corner, and he feels I'm a potential ally. He hopes I'll set the record straight. My conscience forces me to check into his claims to see whether King looked after Berbick's best interests. The promoter was subject to an investigation by the Nevada State Athletic Commission over the division of Berbick's $2.1-million US payday for the Tyson fight. The details remain sketchy, but Berbick reportedly took home only $700,000 US, more than half of which was paid through a letter of credit that may not have been honoured. Was the fight fixed? Probably not. Was Berbick left broken? Without a doubt.

Berbick subsequently lost to Carl (The Truth) Williams, James (Buster) Douglas, Jimmy Thunder, Hasim Rahman, and Lyle McDowell. He also began to turn down fights for bizarre reasons; he decided not to face Joe Bugner in Australia because he was worried about the cold.

His collapse was made even more complete in June 1991, when he was charged with the rape of a family babysitter in Miami. Two months later he forged a cheque for $390.06 US in an act of fiscal desperation. The following month he was charged with armed kidnapping and aggravated assault after he attacked his former financial manager. He allegedly put a gun to her neck and accused her of taking $40,000 US out of his earnings. He was arrested for fraud in December after he forged his wife's signature and took out a $95,000 US mortgage on his Florida home.

In February 1992, he was found guilty of all charges, but the sentencing hearing was delayed. The judge instead asked that Berbick's mental health be evaluated. The order came after Berbick made a rambling speech in the courtroom. Through tears he accused his wife and his lawyer of setting him up. "God will punish you!" he cried. But it was Berbick who was ultimately sentenced to four years in prison. He vanished from radar screens until June 1997, when he was arrested at the airport in Syracuse, New York. He wanted to attend the induction ceremonies at the International Boxing Hall of Fame in nearby Canastota, but the trip constituted a violation of his parole in Florida. As for his boxing records, they had come to an abrupt end — only to resume against the likes of Shane Sutcliffe.

Berbick is excited about the fight. Montreal has always been good to him. He likes to look at Olympic Stadium, where his boxing career first found the mark against John Tate. He says he wants to hear cheering again. He wants to know revenge. "Put yourself in the position of being a fighter," Berbick pleads, making a death-row appeal. "You work so hard to get to the pinnacle, and they tell you to give it up? They take everything from you? But I have seen a light. The door is opening. I've been praying for justice ever since the Tyson fight. Finally, God told me to go for it. I am not going to quit."

He waits for a reaction. I tell him he has my attention. "I've faced too much injustice," he resumes, staring into my eyes. "And I think because of that, God has reached down and given me youth. I am truly blessed. I am not the sustainer of myself. I am not the keeper of myself. God is within me. He makes me supernatural. I am stronger than ever. As fast as I want to be. I can do all things. It may be a long time in coming, but I will be satisfied. God has a way of fixing things up." My tape recorder clicks to a stop. Sixty minutes even. His brother nods, and Berbick pushes his arms through the sleeves of his jacket. He lifts himself gently to his feet, which seem never to touch the ground. I walk, he glides, back to the ballroom that hosted the weigh-in. It's empty. "I guess we'll go home," Berbick says cheerfully. I offer to escort him to the hotel lobby, and we soon find ourselves at the front doors. They're still streaked with rain.

Boxing's history is crowded with men who could have been contenders. There are few fighters, Berbick included, who were. For a moment he watches the rain, and then turns to me and says, "God bless." I shake his hand and say, "Good luck." His eyes light up. "I am looking for God to make some wonderful things happen," he says. "I've got hope."

Trevor Berbick, the former heavyweight champion of the world, again turns his attention to the rain. He wonders aloud how he might get home.

WONDERFUL THINGS

Friday afternoon. Because of deadlines, I have to file a Saturday feature on Berbick before tonight's fight. I write that he's beyond repair and should never be allowed to box again.

The fight is held at the Centre Pierre Charbonneau, a rough-cut arena that can accommodate 3,000 people. It feels like a high-school gym. The place is far from full, but the crowd is drunk and vocal, like strip-club patrons. I have the best seat I've ever had at a fight. I'm seated immediately adjacent to the apron. I can touch the canvas without having to straighten my arm. I watch the undercard fights from a fresh vantage point. I can smell the fighters, feel their heat. I'm sprayed with sweat and a single stream of blood. It stains my shirt. I try to dab it clean with a napkin dunked into Sprite, but I only press the blood more deeply into the fabric. The perils of proximity.

By the time my shirt is dry, Berbick and Sutcliffe are ready to close the show. Berbick enters the arena first. He's wearing his jacket and faded red-and-white trunks. A name he went by for a time, Israel, is stitched across the waistband. The Canadian and Quebec flags have been haphazardly added to each leg. He's also wearing white knee-high socks, like one of the Harlem Globetrotters. Quite an outfit.

His brother Fred walks by his side. Old friends Taylor and Wayne Gordon, a father-and-son team from Halifax, also accompany him. They're in town to work an undercard fight but have volunteered to help out Berbick one final time.

It's a thin crew for a man who used to be Somebody. Still, Berbick acts as though the fans are there to greet him personally, to welcome a favoured son. He jumps up and down as he makes his way to the ring. He blows kisses to the crowd. He playfully bats spectators. The crowd begins to mock him with laughter and jeers. Berbick confuses it with affection. I wince, cursed by unhappy knowledge.

Sutcliffe follows Berbick into the ring. The champion is carried by a small army, dressed uniformly in gold-and-black satin. The crowd cheers. Sutcliffe looks confident as he shakes out his muscled shoulders. He watches with disgust as Berbick does jumping jacks to warm up. Sutcliffe wants to put the old man out to pasture. He knows he's about to fight a living joke.

The opening bell rings. Sutcliffe starts out well. He presses into Berbick and formulates an attack. But Sutcliffe can't land any big punches. Berbick proves impossible to mark. Perhaps he has Tom McCluskey's ancient advice in his mind. His flabby arms, which he keeps high and forward, absorb Sutcliffe's assault. Berbick rarely steps out of his defensive posture. When he does, he uses the opportunity to mock Sutcliffe. Berbick fights with one hand behind his head on occasion. He sticks out his chin. He bows to the referee in response to orders. When the first round comes to a close, he even does the twist on the way to his corner. It has no stool, I notice. Berbick has learned from Sonny Liston to stand between rounds, Don King's poison still coursing through his veins. He rests with his outstretched arms tied around the top ropes. He looks as though he's been crucified.

The fight continues apace. By the fourth round, Sutcliffe looks at Berbick the way the round-card girls watch each other strut on the canvas: both hope the rival will trip and fall. But fall Berbick does not. He begins to hurt Sutcliffe. The champion opens up and starts to bleed from his nose and mouth. The blood turns the white trim on Berbick's trunks a sickly pink. Berbick's white socks are also splattered, but the stains don't come from him. He somehow looks fresh. He scores at will. Inexplicably, the crowd begins to chant: "Ber-bick! Ber-bick! Ber-bick!" He's back where he wants to be. I can't help shaking my head.

Both Sutcliffe and I are licked after the eighth round. I imagine my story rolling on presses across the country: the sorry tale of Trevor Berbick, who, by the way, won the Canadian heavyweight championship last night. How could this be happening? How could I have been so wrong? Fuckity-fuck, I think to myself. Fuckity-fuckity-fuck. The stress makes my eyes burn. Sutcliffe's stare also

★★★TREVOR BERBICK
CELEBRATES AFTER KNOCKING OUT
SHANE SUTCLIFFE. ★★

betrays him during the break. He sits in his corner, weighed down by the burden of impending defeat. His eyes are swollen and filled with hate and despair. Berbick taunts him from across the ring. Sutcliffe slumps deeper into his stool, wishing it would swallow him. His corner shouts instructions into his face, but he appears not to notice. He simply gazes into space. He must know that John Ruiz will remain a stranger. Honky-tonk bars and tough-man competitions, not Madison Square Garden, constitute his new travel plans.

Four pathetic rounds later, as the fight enters its final seconds, Berbick lands two rights to Sutcliffe's skull. Sutcliffe leans against the ropes for support, like a skydiver trapped on telephone wires. The referee moves to end the pounding, but he's too late. Sutcliffe tips forward and falls hard on the canvas with a crack. His face hits the mat and no small amount of blood begins pouring out. The blood looks as black as motor oil. The now former Canadian champion struggles to find his feet. But Sutcliffe's effort is all for nothing. The crowd has a new patsy to tease.

Berbick falls, too. He drops to his knees in the corner closest to me and begins to pray. He rises to his feet and holds his belt — the one he refused to give up so many years ago — high in the steamy air. It's an unbelievable sight. He poses for pictures. He dances with joy. His brother dances beside him. The Gordons stay behind the ropes, but father and son look at each other and begin to laugh. What's so funny? I look at the blood on my shirt and feel myself go green. I take some time to compose myself. But Berbick stays inside the ropes for a long while. He grabs a microphone from a television crew and speaks directly to the camera, unleashing a diatribe. He promises to buy a ranch in Florida for the people of Quebec to use free of charge.

A mixture of hot and cold sweat drips from my face. I decide to climb through the ropes so the evening won't be a total loss: at least I'll know what it's like to be surrounded by cheers. The crowd is obscured by the lights, but its applause filters through the glare, sounding like hail striking a tin roof. The canvas vibrates underfoot. It bounces like a trampoline beneath Berbick, who dances a few feet to my left. I make a cautious approach. His brow is wet, the air around him heavy. He turns to look at me, his eyes burning with a dim fire. He praises the glory of God, his finger pointed skyward. I look at his feet instead and notice a dark stain on the blue canvas. We're standing in a puddle of Sutcliffe's blood. My stomach has hardened by now, like a paramedic's might after a week on the job, and the sight doesn't faze me. But the night's events begin to feel more real. I realize none of the film unspooling before me has been imagined. And I decide Berbick's win is the worst thing that could have happened. It will compound the pain. He'll pursue a futile quest with false hope. He'll be used. He'll confuse greedy attention with love. In different ways, two lives have come crashing down tonight in Montreal. Only in boxing can victory break your heart.

Berbick finally leaves the ring. He's sucked up the last drop of goodness from a disturbing evening. He starts the long walk to his dressing room, and I chase after him. He was alone before the fight, but starry-eyed kids now trail him. They shadowbox and dance behind Berbick but stop at his dressing-room door. I follow Berbick inside. He pulls old clothes out of an orange locker. Taylor Gordon is packing his bags. He still has a bemused smile on his face. He chuckles as Berbick continues to speak without pause about his future glory, the millions of dollars he'll now earn, the joy of sweet, sweet revenge. "I have never felt so much love in all my life," Berbick says. "So much love. So much hope."

I can't listen any longer. I walk across the arena toward Sutcliffe's dressing room. Workers have already started to take down the ring and gather the fold-up chairs. I step gingerly between the tools and piles of swept-up garbage until I reach Sutcliffe's hiding place. I peek inside. He sits on a bench, sobbing deeply. He takes in half-breaths through his clogged nose, his lungs heaving with upset. He picks up a towel and stomps to the showers to be alone.

Yvon Michel, Sutcliffe's manager and chief second, leans against a bank of lockers. "Shane is extremely disappointed," Michel whispers to me. "Berbick's experience showed. In the ring, he looked at home. But it was better for Shane to learn a hard lesson here than in New York." I thank him and leave the dressing room, knowing memories from this night will linger.

I reluctantly return to Berbick's side of the arena. He's showered and dressed. I'm stunned to hear him talking about his upcoming fight against John Ruiz. He says the fight will mark his return to the elite of the heavyweight division. He says he'll regain his rightful title as champion of the world. He earned $10,000 for beating Shane Sutcliffe. Berbick says he won't make the trip to New York for less than $250,000. It's a sum I hope he'll never see.

Berbick can't possibly be allowed to fight Ruiz, who occupies a spot close to the top of the WBC's rankings. I approach Mario Latraverse, the secretary of the WBC, to alleviate my fears. But he confirms that Berbick will likely fight Ruiz. I protest. "We don't have the authority to stop an overage fighter from fighting," Latraverse responds. "Berbick passed all the tests. It's his right. But I can't see us giving him a title shot. Winning in Canada is one thing, but there are some very good fighters in this world. But if he beats Ruiz, who knows?"

I can't believe my ears. I tell Latraverse what will appear in the *National Post* the following morning. He calls me a fool and the insult stings like a cut.

A fool. Convicts respond wildly when they're called goofs. I share their sense of shame and anger. I've heard Berbick's words slur together. I've tapped into a mind racked with paranoia. I've recorded his delusions and boasts and imagined stories. And now I'm the fool?

GUILT

Perhaps Latraverse was right. I've been duped by boxing, drawn close enough to be sucker-punched by Trevor Berbick's sad reality. The champ has left me reeling. I question my easy affection for a sport that routinely leaves men shattered. Until I met Berbick, the fight game's ghosts were fictional for me. Figments of an unkind imagination. But now I know hollow men are out there, armies of old boxers in Reno and Lincoln and Queens, and they can't remember anything except the applause. I replay my conversation with Berbick a few days after returning to Toronto. "I want to hear them chant my name," he said.

I sullied it instead, pulling apart a man whose seams had already come undone. He thought I would help him regain his lost title, trusted me like a friend because I listened. But I heard only a crazy man's dreams. Then I suggested they be erased. I'm not sure he's even read the story, but it doesn't matter. An injustice can be committed against an oblivious victim. My feature on Berbick will earn me high praise, but at what price?

The whole thing continues to eat at me. I have a huge blow-up with my editor that could see me fired. I snap at friends and keep to myself. I can't stop thinking about Berbick. I imagine him at home alone, eating suicide food warmed on a hot plate, dreaming of glory that he'll never taste. Try as I might, I can't shake our shared experience.

I decide to halt my fall into boxing. My happy swing through Vegas is still fresh in my mind, but I have to get out. I'll write about pleasant things, about baseball players who come back from injury and ragtag football teams that score miraculous upsets. The strongest journalists are snitches without remorse (aren't the best stories just rumours held together by scraps of truth?), but I don't want to play that game any longer. No more men lost in fog. No more casinos. No more slot machines. And no more blood. . . .

My self-styled twelve-step program begins on the Yucatán coast in Mexico. I book some time off work, flee south to a resort, and feel better by the middle of my first afternoon away. I sit in the sun, swim in the ocean. I jump into waves and let them slap me on the chest. The water is thick with salt but feels cleansing. I drop myself to the bottom of a forgiving sea.

For some reason, however, I begin reading a boxing book: *A Neutral Corner* by the late A. J. Liebling. It's a mistake. I'm instantly enraptured. His stories have leisure in them, like the ease of a Saturday morning. But beneath the comfort of his work unfolds a familiar struggle. Over the course of the book, he leaves boxing disgusted — "the squalor is now habitual," he says — preferring instead to review something less likely to disappoint, such as war or French restaurants. Of course, he returns to boxing within pages of the breakup, but I ignore his surrender. I'd rather see him as a man who has blazed the trail I'll follow away from prizefighting's spell.

My decision sits well with me, and I enjoy several days of bliss. I withdraw from the world, allow its problems to become foreign to me. The ocean is my only concern.

And then on a hot and glorious Wednesday, I buy the international edition of the *New York Times*. Just for something to read on the beach.

The sun is high. A light wind blows in from the sea. The sports pages, anchored by a bit of sand, flap in the breeze. I pick them up and look at the hockey standings and read the reports from baseball's spring training. I enjoy the fine writing and happily bounce from story to story, scanning each headline until one stops me dead in my tracks: Berbick to be deported from Canada.

Mexico's good work has been for naught.

INNOCENCE

Afflicted with Liebling's curse, I come home with my obsession renewed and immediately check into Berbick's status. A reporter for the Canadian Press named Steve MacLeod has broken the story of Berbick's imminent deportation. It was ordered last summer, but Berbick was still a has-been then. He wasn't news. When MacLeod read my story, I presume, he decided to investigate matters further and won himself a scoop. I made a rookie mistake in assuming Berbick was a Canadian citizen. He's actually a landed immigrant, but his convictions in Florida mean he's ineligible for continued residency. He's being sent home to Jamaica. Goddamn.

Not only was my story a cheap shot, but it was incomplete, too. The case has wide implications. Boxing authorities have been caught off guard. They also assumed Berbick was either a Canadian citizen or a legal resident. A national embarrassment — our heavyweight champion is a forty-something-year-old head case — has become an outright debacle. If Berbick's immigration status had been made public earlier, his fight against Sutcliffe would not have been sanctioned. Perhaps Sutcliffe would have beaten another fighter and still kept his date with John Ruiz. And Berbick would not have been filled with groundless hope. Now disappointment awaits him, even though it's good news in a bitter sense. Berbick's legal problems mean that Ruiz will dance with another partner in New York. An execution has been postponed by a handcuffed trip home.

But Berbick has appealed the order. A hearing into the matter will be held. Canadian boxing officials say Berbick will be stripped of the crown if he's deported; if he's allowed to stay, he'll keep the title.

Steve MacLeod continues to dig in the meantime. He quickly issues another blow to Berbick, revealing that he's wanted by authorities in Florida for breaking his parole. A warrant for his arrest was issued after Berbick failed to meet with his stateside peace officer. MacLeod calls Berbick to ask about the transgression. He denies breaking probation. "I did everything," he says. "All this is untrue. It is a misunderstanding. You guys treat me like I'm some kind of foreigner. What you're trying to do is destroy me as a black man." Berbick must have read my story after all.

The deportation hearing is delayed, and the venue shifts from Halifax to Montreal before it's belatedly called to order. I want to attend, but the *National Post* sends Roy MacGregor, our national affairs columnist. Maybe I'm too close to the story to do it justice.

Seven weeks later, on December 1, 1999, the decision arrives at the *Post* via the fax machine. I watch as a dozen pages roll out. I can't look at them until the machine clicks to a pause, like a poker player who refuses to pick up his cards until all five are dealt. I don't want to jinx things. "Décision Berbick," the first page reads.

Analysis follows. I flip to the conclusion. "The deportation of the appellant from Canada would not serve the interests of justice," it begins. Berbick has been saved by the testimony of Reverend Darryl G. Louis Grey of the United Church of Canada; Dan Philip, the president of the Black Coalition of Quebec; and three young boxers who called him an inspiration and "the pride of our gym."

"He leads an active life in the boxing area here in Canada," the decision continues. "He appears to act as a mentor to young boxers, and according to credible witnesses, could be usefully involved in helping the youth. The tribunal, after having considered the totality of the evidence, concludes the appellant has discharged the burden of proof and considering all the circumstances of the case, a five-year stay, with the conditions attached hereto, is appropriate." In sum, Berbick will have to keep clean for five years and then he's a free man, eligible for Canadian citizenship.

At his press conference, Berbick beams. "It means a lot to me," he says of the decision, "because my dream, my goal, is to continue to fight and to win back the heavyweight championship of the world. Spirit don't have no age, and I am a spirit. I'm gonna be the champ again. Check it out, man," he yells. "I am a living miracle!" Berbick thrusts his fist high in the air. Guilty no longer, I follow suit.

BOXING TAKES ONE ON THE CHIN

★ LENNOX LEWIS V. EVANDER HOLYFIELD ★

MARCH 13, 1999

Then we said goodbye to the gang, and night was falling as we left Harlem. Jack was unusually quiet for a while as we drove back past the boarded-up streets. But then he lit up another cigar, adjusted his titfer to its normally jaunty angle, sighed and said, "Amazing, it's all changed. But at least we met some nice fellas."

— JONATHAN RENDALL, *THIS BLOODY MARY IS THE LAST THING I OWN*

THE CHELSEA HOTEL

The worst thing for a recovering addict is the promise of a best-ever hit. I haven't fully rid myself of Trevor Berbick's misery when I'm given a ticket to the heavyweight championship of the world. Lennox Lewis and Evander Holyfield will unify the title at boxing's mecca, and I'm asked to join them. It's too tempting an offer to refuse. I board the plane consumed by a strange kind of joy, a sort of happy reluctance, like a boy who's always wanted to drive suddenly being handed the wheel. Worry pangs accompany my arrival in Gotham, the dread that only sellouts know.

A yellow cab drops me in front of the landmark Chelsea Hotel. It stands at 222 West 23rd Street, south and west of the Empire State Building. Bronze plaques surround the heavy front door, informing passersby that Dylan Thomas drank himself to death here. Thomas Wolfe stayed here. So, too, did Arthur Miller, O. Henry, Mark Twain, and William S. Burroughs. Arthur C. Clarke wrote *2001: A Space Odyssey* in one of the rooms. Virgil Thomson and Bob Dylan and Patti Smith made music here. Nancy Spungen died in room 100, and Sid Vicious took the blame. Woody Allen filmed *Manhattan Murder Mystery* in the maze-like hallways. And Leonard Cohen was serviced by Janis Joplin on one of its ancient beds. No plaque commemorates the famous blowjob, but Cohen tips his hat to Joplin's kindness in "Chelsea Hotel No. 2" ("Giving me head on the unmade bed . . .").

I hope the hotel will treat me equally well. I've heard it's dumpy but friendly, a good home for creative types and locos. It's also cheap by New York standards — only 150 bills per night. My editor gladly feeds my desire to reside in dives whenever I go on the road. I like to think that my stories come out darker and more dramatic when the bedsheets reek of sweat and exposed lightbulbs dangle from smoke-stained ceilings.

I walk through the front doors and see a fireplace filling one wall. The rest are covered with the refuse of crazed minds. Paintings that resemble crime scenes leave little naked space. Strange sculptures made of plastic and sharp metal occupy windowsills and tabletops. A life-sized plaster figure sits on a swing, suspended from the lobby ceiling.

The front desk is virtually hidden beneath the clutter. A massive man with arms as long as my legs stands behind it. Dressed in black, he cuts a formidable figure for a front-desk clerk, but he gives me a discount because I'm staying for six nights. "Bulk rate," he says with a smile.

He offers to escort me to my room, and I welcome the prospect of a guard. We step into the tiny, creaky elevator, which slowly finds its way to the fifth floor. More art covers the walls in the hallway. I follow my guide as he makes several turns around corners and through cobwebs until we arrive at an unmarked door painted brown. "Your room," he says, sliding the key into the lock.

The bed is next to the door. An old television sits on the other side of the bed, between two tall windows protected by white shutters and dusty drapes. A relic of a clock radio turns over on the nightstand. A desk-dresser combination is pushed against the far wall, next to a rusted radiator and adjacent to the bathroom door. The ceiling is high, and there's a step up to access the commode. It appears held together only by its pipes, but it functions well enough. A thin frosted window is next to the toilet. I examine the basin for condoms and syringes. Nada. The day's last light is reflected in the porcelain. A good sign. I will not drown in the dark as Dylan Thomas did.

I return to the bedroom and tug at the window shutters. They're heavy with thick layers of paint but crack open to reveal something close to a view. I'm just high enough to peer over neighbouring rooftops. Chelsea, the district, feels a little like a movie set. The streets are relatively narrow, and the buildings are old and carbon-covered, packed tightly together, and many of them boast turn-of-the-century water towers and chimneys silhouetted by the setting sun. I imagine I'm in Hell's Kitchen in the 1930s, wearing a wife-beater and yelling insults out the window — "Will you people shaddup already!"

I turn on the television but it doesn't work, so I call the front desk. The man in black returns, looks at the television sternly, jiggles a few connections, and smacks the box once on its side. It flickers to life. I smile and thank him. He decides to show me how to turn the radiator on and off. Spring might have arrived, he says, but the nights are still cool. I thank him again.

I put on the radiator, as instructed, and turn out the lights before turning in. The pipes expand and begin to bang, metal on metal, with every blast of heat. I lie awake and listen to the ghostly lullaby, thinking about the giants who have shared the same roof. I think about Leonard Cohen especially.

HYPE

Prior to his impending fight against Lennox Lewis, Evander Holyfield lays claim to the IBF and WBA titles. Lewis owns the WBC crown. Thus the match will witness the unification of all three belts. Boxing hasn't witnessed an all-the-marbles heavyweight fight since Mike Tyson beat Tony Tucker in 1987. And there hasn't been a unified heavyweight champion since 1992, when Riddick Bowe threw the WBC belt in the trash rather than face Lewis. Boxing's glamour division has been in disarray since. But there will be no more confusion. One hero will stand alone. Don King, the fight's evangelical promoter, is billing the event as "The unmitigated, unadulterated, undisputed heavyweight championship of the world!"

I wake to a cold morning and hope he's right. The dull roar of traffic trickles through the windows, but the bustle seems calm next to the pre-fight press conference. It's held in a theatre at Madison

Square Garden, the fabled arena and home to the fight. The stage has been set. Two rows of raised tables and two dozen chairs await the fight's principal actors. A microphone is perched on the middle of the platform. A long row of cameras and photographers forms a breakwater not far from the edge of the stage. Reporters crowd the leftover space either immediately in front of the stage or in the seats behind the cameras. They chat and scribble notes in a hundred different dialects. Most of them glisten with a thin sheen of sweat. The room is already warm, and the spotlights have not yet been fired up.

They will shine most brightly on Holyfield, the American. Yanks look at boxing's biggest championship the way they view liberty or cheap gas by the gallon: such things are American birthrights, and you'd best be ready for a fight should you want to take them away. But Lewis is the better story for my money. He once called himself a Canadian — he brought a gold medal home to Canada from the 1988 Olympics in Seoul — and is a far more interesting character than Holyfield. Evander is a religious man who offers only a series of polite, deferential clichés when interviewed. He gives a great deal of thanks to God and quotes the Bible. Lewis, who now carries the flag of Great Britain, is also quiet, but something more ticks inside his head. Lewis is illiterate but intelligent; a big boy who still clings to his mother. He excels in a brute's business but likes nothing more than a good game of chess.

Lewis is also burdened by a number of bad raps, and his struggle makes for good copy. Most boxing writers, particularly Americans, have always seen something soft in him, and there are persistent accusations that he ducks hard opposition. Rumours also abound that he's gay, and hostile reporters berate Lewis with a subtle homophobia. "Lewis doesn't have the intestinal fortitude," they write. "He lacks the necessary killer instinct." Lewis does not take kindly to the bashing. A reporter once asked him about his courage on the canvas. Lewis responded, "I'm 100 percent a ladies' man, don't you worry about that." It seemed a strange answer at the time, but Lewis wanted to cut to the chase: a man who plays chess isn't queer by default.

His muddy heritage acts as a further hindrance. Lewis was born in London to Jamaican parents. He moved to Canada with his mother as a twelve-year-old. He fought as an amateur on behalf of Canada but established himself as a professional boxer on the other side of the pond. His accent is ambiguous; his history serves only to confuse. American fight fans like neither mystery nor mutts. They're more happy with the Pittsburgh Kid and the Brown Bomber and That Damn Jew. Labels make picking sides a simple proposition. Unfortunately for Lewis, he's impossible to typecast. His lack of identity makes him tough to market. Even Britons aren't quite sure what to make of him. Lewis is a man without a home.

Holyfield, on the other hand, was born, raised, and continues to live in Atlanta, Georgia. His place in history is equally secure. *The Ring* magazine has called Holyfield the third-best heavyweight of all time, behind only Muhammad Ali and Joe Louis. He was a 25-to-1 underdog before his first fight with Tyson, but he dismantled Iron Mike in eleven rounds. He was on his way to beating Tyson a second time when he had his ear chewed off. Holyfield also engaged in three wars with the beefy Bowe. He lost twice, once by decision and once by an eighth-round TKO, but he won the second meeting on points after a courageous performance. The victory justified his reputation as The Warrior and won him the WBA and IBF titles. Though he would lose them to Michael Moorer in 1994, Holyfield later recovered from his trio of defeats and regained his belts. Now Holyfield will put them on the line once again, with confidence firmly in his corner.

But first, the two men make their way to the theatre. Lewis stands a head taller than everyone else on the stage. His dreadlocks are tucked under a black cap. He looks calm. Holyfield wears the serene smile of a man with nothing left to prove. He acts as though the heavyweight belts are his by divine right. Only Don King looks to be excited. He possesses a rich man's glow. He hoots and hollers

★★★SHOCK-HAIRED HUCKSTER DON KING HEDGES HIS BETS PRIOR TO HOLYFIELD-LEWIS

★★★★★★

before the festivities begin. His deep voice carries across the room without the aid of amplifiers.

In the days prior to the press conference, Holyfield and Lewis have been vocal as well. Neither man is known for his vicious oratory, but each has lashed out at the other. Holyfield, who has never before predicted the outcome of a fight, said he would knock out Lewis in the third round, calling it God's will. Lewis laughed at the suggestion and dismissed Holyfield as a hypocrite. His aim was true. Despite his religious convictions, Holyfield has fathered at least five children out of wedlock, and perhaps as many as seven. Even Holyfield doesn't seem to know exactly how many offspring he has sired. But the link between his private life and public face displeased Holyfield. He will seek vengeance in the ring, he said. Lewis taunted him again: "I'm the best heavyweight on the planet, period."

Yet both men appear to have a change of heart once the press conference gets underway. They try to downplay any friction, and it doesn't make for a memorable afternoon. Lewis is the first to soften his stance. "A lot is being made about what I said about Evander," he begins, "about him being a hypocrite. I've seen Evander say on TV that a hypocrite to him is somebody who is a quitter. I never said he is a hypo-quit. I just want to make that clear." He continues: "I've done a lot of talking now. I need to do my talking in the ring. I will walk into the ring with one belt and will walk out with three. It's time to just think about the fight. I'll let my hands do the talking. I will be victorious." Lewis has never been one to provide illuminating quotations. But this pre-fight performance is a personal worst.

Holyfield, too, sounds apologetic rather than apoplectic: "I know that a lot of things have been said. A lot of people have been surprised by what I said. Lennox is tough. He is a champion. I don't take that away from him. I'm not going to sit here and drag somebody down. But I'm going to knock him out. He's going to fight a good fight. But he's going to fall short. I'm fighting a guy who is worthy. But I'm still the head. Lennox is the neck. He's just a little bit lower than me."

It's up to Don King to save the day. He doesn't disappoint. His promotion has already sold out, but he adds still more electricity to the hyperbolic chamber. He speaks for seventy-six consecutive minutes, introducing every person on the stage with effusive affection; I wonder whether he'll tearfully thank the janitors who wait to clean up the day's debris. King also manages to roll Shakespeare, NATO, Bill Clinton, the Bosnian conflict, a few passages from the Bible, Henry VIII, and Henry Kissinger into his speech. "The unmitigated, unadulterated, undisputed heavyweight championship of the world!" he repeats. "History in the making! Live on pay-per-view! Call your local cable company!" It's a fine display. But the room exhales in relief when King finally steps from the stage. To paraphrase Reggie Jackson, even ice cream can taste bad when it's stuffed down your throat.

King's marathon leaves me little time before deadline. I need to file 700 words on the press conference in less than an hour. I pull out my computer and begin banging away on a table set up close to the stage. About ten other reporters get the same idea. Our fingers dance rapidly, but the clack-clack-clack of our keyboards is drowned out by the ongoing ruckus in the theatre.

Television reporters send live feeds over the ocean. Radio correspondents — the BBC World Service is within a stone's throw — call in their reports. Print reporters scramble for one-on-one interviews they'll never receive. Hangers-on hang on. The marginal characters that float around boxing try to act important. They greet each other with puffed chests and secret handshakes that say, "Like you, my brother, I add no value to this glorious game." I'm trying to write in the chaos of the newsroom times ten. But boxing has its own peculiar pressures. You're never quite sure when someone might look over your shoulder, take exception to your approach, and plunge a screwdriver into the back of your skull.

The stress does not make for good work. My story is becoming a mess. The din makes it hard to see a train of thought through to its conclusion. I flip madly through my notebook in a fruitless search for quality quotes. Unless you're on death row, time always flies when you're desperate for more.

Much to my dismay, Don King makes his way toward the tables. He sits down immediately across from me. He looks weary. He dabs a handkerchief across his brow and rubs the part of his nose that supports his thick glasses. An assistant carries two fistfuls of cellular phones. King takes a moment to catch his breath. I continue to work on my story. Fifteen more minutes. The assistant passes one of the phones to King. It's a far-away radio station on the line. King suddenly lights up and gives the people what they want. Another phone is passed to him and the conversation is repeated. Then another. And another. The assistant handles the incoming calls like a taxi dispatcher. King finishes with one phone and the next is planted on his ear. He juggles with his mouth. He never drops the ball, but it remains impossible for me to concentrate. My time is up. I send the story to the newsroom both late and lame.

I lean back in my chair, my supply of adrenaline tapped out. King has found a reserve of energy. He keeps on working the phones. An endless parade of media outlets demands his time. It seems as though the whole world has taken notice of this fight. Evander Holyfield and Lennox Lewis have failed to talk the talk, but they've promised to make noise when it matters. What a night it is going to be.

BERT SUGAR AND THE CRYING GIRL

A man from HBO approaches another Toronto reporter, Steve Simmons, and me after we've filed our stories from the press conference. He gives us passes to a party that evening. "An exclusive to boxing writers," the black type reads.

The party is in the basement of a Manhattan bar, and it's as chaotic as the cafeteria at fat camp. We check our coats at the top of the stairs. Two young girls stand nearby. They look underage.

They want desperately to know what's happening downstairs. "I'm sure we'll see them later," I say to Steve. He smiles. We head below ground.

About seventy writers, all of them men, are packed into the place. Sixty-five are smoking. There's heaps of food. A bartender pulls free pints. I'm soon full and drunk. Steve and I circulate among reporters from across North America before Don King arrives with a couple of bodyguards and holds court. A huddle forms around him as he continues his running battle with the New York press, an endless saga. I'm not distracted from the debate until the two girls from the top of the stairs make the trip down. One is sexy in a one-night-stand sort of way: big hair and big boobs. The other will never be pretty, no matter how many pints I put back.

Adding teenage girls to that room is like spilling blood in shark-infested waters. Most of the reporters leave King and set their sights. I lean against a wall and watch the dance. It reminds me of the first round of a fight. The hot chick laps up the attention. The ugly one wonders when her turn might come.

Without warning, Big Hair breaks away from her suitors and walks toward me. She looks into my eyes. My heart beats faster. She smiles and extends her hand. I shake it. "I really like your sideburns," she says. "Thanks," I say. The other writers watch with their mouths wide open. They're about to be outscored by a kid. The girl leans in. I think she's going to kiss me, but she lunges for my ear: "My friend really likes you," she purrs. "She thinks you're cute. You should make a move." She smiles again and returns to the middle of the pack. I'm crestfallen. A thick line divides studs from grenade catchers. I don't want to take one for the team.

The beer earns my affection instead. I down a few more pints. I'm well and truly shining. I talk to hammered strangers as though I've known them all my life. Then a commotion hits the floor. Ugly Girl has burst into tears. Now dubbed Crying Girl, she flees to a corner of the room. We probably should try to make her feel better, but our circle remains intact. We turn cold shoulders. Our crew has little patience for false drama.

But a man named Bert Sugar sees an opening. The veteran writer and boxing historian has one of the sport's most recognizable mugs. He's somewhere between sixty and one hundred years old. He's as bald as a coot and wears a fedora to cover his dome. His eyes are sunken behind a bulbous nose, and a cigar is forever stuffed into his black, wet mouth. Sugar wears clothes that match his outdated personality. Doesn't talk so much as bark, and most of it is filth. We all know Sugar will want something from the girl in exchange for his sympathy. And we know he won't be satisfied with a hug. A bad situation is about to be made worse.

Sugar sits beside Crying Girl and begins stroking her long hair. He leans close to her face and nuzzles her neck. He whispers into her ear and puts a hand on her leg. The girl keeps sobbing. The room begins to go still. I look at Steve. He looks at me. Maybe it's time to step in. But Sugar takes to his feet with a flourish. "He's dead!" he yells at the girl. "D-E-A-D! Dead! Do you hear me? Nothing is going to bring him back. Nothing. I'll spell it out for you again: D-E-A-D! He's fuckin' dead!" Sugar storms toward the bar.

Emboldened by drink, I decide to block his path. He looks at me as if to say, "Problem?" "What was that all about, Bert?" I ask. He repeats what he's just said to the girl, complete with the spelling lesson. He hacks out each letter like a hairball. "Yeah, Bert, I know what you said. But who are you talking about? Who's dead?"

"Aw," Sugar says. "Her fuckin' dad."

"What? When did he die?"

"I dunno. A few days ago. She's still carrying a picture of him around. Like I need to see that. I told her she just needs to get over it. Crying's no good for nobody."

Sugar orders a frosty cocktail. It's a few degrees warmer than he is. I ask for another pint, and the room is empty by the time I finish it. Big Hair and Crying Girl have left without company. I go back to the Chelsea and the radiator lulls me to sleep, banging in time to the pounding in my head.

LIGHTWEIGHT

Fortunately, the weigh-in is not until the following afternoon. I need the morning to recover. But my night of drinking with kingpins has left me feeling like a player. I exit the lobby of the Chelsea Hotel and join the sidewalk crowds with ego's spring in my step.

My sense of privilege disappears after the long walk up Seventh Avenue to Madison Square Garden. I arrive well before the weigh-in and decide to pick up my fight pass. A desk has been set up inside one of the rear entrances. Several boxes sit on top of it. A nice woman behind the desk asks for my name. "Jones," I say. "Chris." She opens a box labelled F–J. It contains hundreds of passes. She pulls out three stamped with my name alone. She asks for my affiliation. "The *National Post*," I say. "From Toronto." She hands me one of the three passes. It's marked with the worst possible word: "Auxiliary." I feel something close to shame. The designation means I won't be seated at ringside (those passes bear the word "Ring") and perhaps not even within the arena itself. I'll be among the scrubs and nobodies, and I dread watching the fight on a television buried in the basement, a custom normally reserved for mega-events such as the Super Bowl. This must be a mistake. I ask the woman how many members of the media have been accredited. "1,961," she replies. My heart sinks as I commit the number to memory.

I make out like a small fish and swim toward the media centre. A good chunk of the Garden's cold lower concourse is filled with dozens of fold-up tables. Six chairs sit behind each one. The tables are decorated with numerous phones and face an impressive array of television monitors; I hope again that I won't have to watch the fight on them. Writers have laid claim to particular spots with laptop computers, empty coffee cups, and plates of half-finished food. A few guys sit working. Others gather in small groups and make predictions, spread gossip. I don't care to join them and continue to nose around. The media centre is separated by blue curtains from the area that will hold the post-fight press conference. Hundreds of chairs face the stark stage erected there. Another area, again cordoned off by blue curtains, holds fax and Telex machines that ring continuously. Copies of press releases and newspaper clippings are piled next to them. Several sheets of paper have fallen from the tables and litter the polished concrete floor. It looks like a miniature stock exchange in late afternoon, but our day's trading has just begun.

I find my way back to the Garden's main theatre. A scale has replaced the dais and microphone on the stage. The rest of the scene remains unchanged from the previous afternoon. Cameramen and photographers assume their usual positions; reporters fill the spaces in between; Don King's henchmen, dressed in black-and-white jackets with the words "Only in America" emblazoned across each of their backs, do their best to keep order. The air fills with mundane conversation and idle speculation. The temperature in the room begins to rise as 1,961 reporters make their way to the show. I wonder where Chris Jones 2 and Chris Jones 3 are. Perhaps I can roll them for a good seat.

My nasty thoughts are interrupted when Lennox Lewis appears. The stage is crowded with commissioners and officials and wastes of skin, but Lewis towers above the rabble. His dreadlocks are again stuffed into a black knit cap, but this time the brand name FCUK is inscribed on the front in white thread. Most of us look twice at the logo. Lewis strips down to his underwear and panics the scale. His arms are long and thick and conclude with two significant fists. His chest is broad, his stomach tight with bundles of muscle. His legs are also finely cut. Even his feet look strong. Lewis smiles and flexes his biceps for the cameras when his weight is announced. He comes in at 246 pounds. Not one ounce of it is fat.

Evander Holyfield then emerges from the crowd on the stage, though he can't be made out clearly until he stands alone on the scale. Holyfield would be a big man on the streets, but he's small next to Lewis. He weighs only 215 hard-won pounds. His thin legs provide some indication of his body's natural lines. Holyfield began his boxing career as a greyhound; he weighed 177 pounds before his first professional fight in 1984. The additional weight was acquired via unknown means. At thirty-six, Holyfield should be past his physical peak. But his chest and neck remain stretched to the breaking point, as if he'd been stung by bees. The servant of God is well-sculpted.

Still, Holyfield looks poorly equipped for his fight with Lewis. It smacks of a sucker's bet. Holyfield's trainer, a small man named Don Turner, tried earlier to minimize the matter of size. "What difference does it make?" he asked reporters. "[Rocky] Marciano gave away pounds to every fighter he fought. What difference does that make? A guy that weighs 180 pounds can hurt anybody." But while the biggest man does not always come out on top, it's never easy to get inside a boxer much larger than you are.

There is no shortage of observers ignorant to biology, however. The American press (the New York tabloids in particular) continues to dismiss Lewis as yellow. The gambling community is also on Holyfield's side. The odds on a third-round knockout, Holyfield's predicted outcome to the fight, drop from 30–1 to 15–1 virtually overnight. A man who gives away thirty-one pounds to his opponent somehow remains the heavy favourite. I decide boxing writers and bookies would be lousy at choosing sides in a bar fight.

After Holyfield and Lewis depart from the stage without so much as a word, reporters mill about the theatre floor looking for crumbs. I slip into a circle of Gotham pressmen. One of the reporters is caught in the middle of a roast by his colleagues. They make fun of the consistently negative tone of his work. He feigns hurt feelings and offers a telling response: "That's not true," he complains. "I wrote something positive today, didn't you see? I wrote that Holyfield is going to knock Lewis flat." The group laughs and I figure a quick smile will help me fit in. A few of the older men look toward me. The reporter closest to me glances at the pass dangling around my neck. He smirks and takes a small step to his left. It doesn't matter that I write for a national newspaper in Canada, or that I've taken drinks with Don King and Bert Sugar, or that I'm spending the night at the Chelsea Hotel. I have been labelled auxiliary, and a fat man in a bad jacket has shut me out.

NEW YORK SHITTY

Boxing has been similarly shunned for some time in New York. Its affection for the sport seems to rise when the city's fortunes dim, and vice versa: when the city prospers, boxing's prospects are less bright. New York is in the midst of a boom as Evander Holyfield and Lennox Lewis prepare to meet. Thus the sport is on the ropes.

I need to find a part of the city where a champion's crowning remains an event, where I can feel a sense of occasion. The Kingsway International Boxing Club, one of the last gyms in Manhattan, fits the bill. Rising rents have forced many downtown clubs to close. But the Kingsway has kept a tenuous grip on the second floor of an old brick building near the corner of 28th Street and Broadway. The shadow of the Empire State Building crosses the street not far to the east. The skyscraper looms over the Kingsway like a volcano about to erupt.

A narrow staircase provides access to the club's single ring and its collection of heavy bags and medicine balls. It looks a bit like a movie set awaiting the arrival of Clubber Lang or The Champ. A black man with high cheekbones sits behind a cluttered desk in a quiet corner. He's on the phone. We nod at each other. I scan the gym as I wait. Two young fighters are working out. One jumps rope as though a bomb will go off the instant he stops. The other paws a speed bag with gentle jabs. He has a selective look in his eyes as he throws his well-timed punches, like a man picking only the ripest fruit from a tree.

The man on the phone hangs it up and wanders over to greet me. He looks welcoming but skeptical: just another kid who'll work out twice and disappear. As I take his hand the mileage of many years rubs against my skin, but his face is tight and proud. I introduce myself as a reporter. "Michael Olajide," he says with a smile. "What can I do for you?"

"The New York boxing scene," I answer. "I want to talk to you about it."

He smiles again as he puts his hand on my back and guides me toward his desk. He begins to excavate a chair from piles of paper and photographs. Before he's finished, I notice a newspaper profile on the wall. It is illustrated with an old picture of a young man, Olajide long ago.

"You were a fighter?" I ask.

"Lightweight," he responds. "I was once ranked seventh in the world, when I was the champion of Nigeria. You?"

I shake my head, embarrassed, like I don't belong in his company because I've never passed boxing's most brutal initiation. He senses my discomfort and asks me where I'm from. "Canada," I tell him.

"Ah," he lights up. "I lived in Vancouver. But my son was a fighter, a middleweight, and he would go nowhere in Vancouver. We had to come here."

I accept the opening and ask Olajide about his gym, how long he'd been neighbours with the Empire State Building. "This is not where I started," he says. "I used to be up at 40th and Eighth. But rents kept going up, and I didn't have enough fighters, so I had to move down here." He didn't need to elaborate. I already knew his story. A.J. Liebling told it well.

In *A Neutral Corner*, the book I'd read on Mexico's beaches, Liebling offers a detailed account of boxing's death in New York, like a crime writer documenting a murder. Gotham, he laments, was once heavily populated with small boxing gyms and clubs. Nothing fancy, but places where fans could get a fix of violence at close quarters and journeymen could earn a decent living. "There were once a lot of boxing gyms here," confirms Olajide. "There were about sixty clubs in Manhattan when I came to town, everywhere, like corner shops."

Change came rapidly with television. Popular fighters were awarded silk purses, but the local clubs lost much of their combined gate to the networks, and a hothouse vanished with every satellite sent into space. Liebling writes about the disappearance of penny fights in exchange for million-dollar shows. Ringside seats became a luxury enjoyed only by celebrities and the well-connected.

Cigarettes made way for cigars. Boxing, Liebling concludes, was marginalized by its own success.

"Now there are no more than a dozen clubs in Manhattan," says Olajide. "They just began closing down, closing down, closing down. We're just lucky they haven't been able to sweat us out." Few could make the same boast.

The Times Square Gym, a rough but esteemed school, closed down when Disney and company began to push the porn shops and peep shows out of the city's heart: both boxers and strippers had to find a new home. Stillman's, the so-called University of Eighth Avenue, has also disappeared. (A shoe-repair shop took its place.) Even Gleason's, New York's best gym according to Michael Katz, couldn't keep its hold on 30th Street. It moved across the river to Brooklyn. "New York used to be the mecca of boxing," Olajide sighed. "Not anymore. But maybe once again."

Olajide, it seems, has great faith in the healing powers of Holyfield v. Lewis. But I protest: "There are so many other distractions here. Boxing doesn't seem to matter."

He lifts his hand to stop me. "You'll see," Olajide says. "It will, my friend. Oh, it will be something."

He presents hard evidence to back his case. More than 20,000 spectators will fill a sold-out Madison Square Garden, Olajide says, and scalpers are putting ringside seats on the block for close to ten grand. Still, I remain skeptical. In places such as Mashantucket or Montreal, a big fight consumes the city. I had known the ring as epicentre. But New Yorkers have gone almost thirty years without a Main Event. "Will they find their appetite again?" I ask.

Olajide assumes the patient look of a teacher. "The fights, they always happen in Las Vegas or Atlantic City," he explains, referring to the casino money that drives the fight game. "But this is the biggest fight in a long time, and we've got it. A lot of people who may have forgotten about boxing may get into it again. I know they will." Olajide puts his hands behind his head and leans back. He smiles an easy smile. "This is good," he says. "This is very, very good." Maybe a few more kids will be inspired to join his club, he says. If not, Olajide can still point to the $20 million US Holyfield will take home, or to the $10 million US Lewis will pocket, and his existing stable will work harder, put in a few more miles of roadwork, pound the bags like men possessed.

Olajide rises from behind his desk to underscore the point. He admonishes one of his pupils, the lean man jumping rope, for being out of condition. He has to take things more seriously, Olajide counsels. If he wants to be like Evander Holyfield, if he wants to be like Lennox Lewis, if he wants to fight at Madison Square Garden under the gaze of the world, he will have to step it up. The man at the speed bag stops to listen to the sermon. He resumes his work with renewed interest, watched by portraits of Muhammad Ali and George Foreman, Rocky Marciano and Mike Tyson. The stern faces are painted directly onto the brick with quick, kinetic brushstrokes. The images stick with me as I walk back to the Chelsea. I turn them over in my mind and feel my earlier opinion soften. Saturday night might make like smelling salts, reviving New York from its selfish stupor. Michael Olajide has every right to harbour optimism after all.

Because at the Kingsway, at the Westside Gym in Washington Heights, at the Waterfront Club by the piers, heavyweight champions have never been taken lightly.

MADISON SQUARE GARDEN

Evander Holyfield and Lennox Lewis relax at their hotels the day before the fight. No official events are scheduled. I decide to get my bearings before the Garden fills with thousands of drunk and rabid fans. I go to the media centre and ask whether I have a confirmed seat. I do. A helpful woman produces a map of the arena and points out my section. It doesn't look promising, but I'm relieved nonetheless. I find my way into the Garden's upper bowl, the air cool from the hockey rink shining white below. I climb several more flights of concrete stairs. My seat is at the end of the last row, tucked close to the corner most distant from ringside. I still haven't paid my dues.

I sit on my perch. The Garden is empty aside from a small group of hockey parents watching their children. Tiny blades follow the deep cuts left by idols. It's a spirited contest — the tykes from Greenwich and the New York Stars act like long-time rivals — but I grow tired of not being able to see the puck for the distance.

My eyes drift toward the roof. I'm struck by the absence of rafters. Arenas are normally capped with a web of exposed steel, but Madison Square Garden must have the construction of a tent instead. The roof is sunken in the middle, as though King Kong sat on it after he finished with Fay Wray. On first appearances it looks to be made of wood. In fact, something close to aluminum siding has been slatted between dozens of black metal pipes that converge above the score clock. The pipes, because they shoot outward from the building's centre, add to the illusion that the roof is about to collapse.

Immediately beneath the roof are rows of luxury boxes. A shallow balcony of cheap seats starts below them, and the lower bowl fills the rest of the space. The layout is more circular than most arenas, which tend to be oval or rectangular. The seats are also a departure from the norm. They are teal and purple like chairs in a kindergarten classroom, and lend a decidedly lighthearted feel to a building associated primarily with battle.

The kids finish up. I return to the press centre for a couple of hours. The media army is now firmly encamped; it will not leave until a war story is written. The place is much more hectic than it was earlier in the week. Areas where I walked freely before are suddenly off-limits. The piles of press releases are quickly snapped up. The hum of laptops is louder now, and the floor is wet with spilled drinks and perspiration. I assemble a dinner from a complimentary buffet and pick up a free pass to that night's hockey game: New York Rangers v. Boston Bruins.

The game lasts more than three hours, but all signs of it are erased soon afterward. Workers immediately begin to prepare the arena for the fight, laying down tarps and protective flooring on top of the rink. It's difficult to remove blood when it freezes to ice.

GOD SAVE THE REST OF US

I pay ten bucks to rent a pair of binoculars from a concession stand in the Madison Square Garden concourse. The place is crowded with fight fans. Almost 22,000 people have packed the arena, including a considerable contingent from the UK. Most of the Britons are seated with me in the arena's upper reaches. The lower bowl is filled with Americans who didn't have to pay for a flight as well as their ticket. Even the grandstands are set up for a confrontation.

The Britons occupy themselves during the tedious undercard with flag-waving and fight songs. I was worried earlier that I would miss out on the energy of the ring because of my bad seat, but my companions make up for the gulf. The chants of the English fans wash across the arena, rebounding off the far wall and back again. The energy is palpable and the noise close to deafening. The Main Event is still hours away, but it's impossible to hear my immediate neighbours — writers from the *Kansas City Star* and *Palm Beach Post* — unless they holler at the top of their lungs.

I cast my eyes across the bowl, finding something ugly about the crowd. It reminds me of the Mike Tyson fans in Las Vegas, a collection of hair-triggers. There's a hooligan element milling about the aisles. Their ranks seem to swell with every chorus of song. England's foot-soldiers are ready for battle. Many take drunken stumbles down the stairs between each section of seats, but they remain a hard lot. I'm on edge. My hands leave my computer only to scratch out a scorecard, my first, on a blank sheet of paper; only now do I feel confident enough to judge a fight. I put an L and an H at the top of the page and write the number of each round down the left-hand margin. I stop at the sixth. I decide the fight will end then. It had better not go the distance. I don't want to be among the thugs after twelve rounds of drink.

Unfortunately, the evening kicks off badly for the Britons — and for those who fear them — when England's Howard Clarke loses on the undercard to (Ferocious) Fernando Vargas. The referee stops the title fight after Clarke's Union Jack trunks are burned by the canvas four times in the fourth round alone. The UK boys still feel the stoppage is an affront to their manhood. An entire nation takes offence because a favourite son is unable to stay on his feet. Abuse and epithets are hurled toward the ring, the visitors making it clear that they will not accept defeat.

And they have no desire for quiet. When Lennox Lewis enters the arena, I wonder whether the Garden's sunken roof will blow off. It's the loudest ovation I've ever heard, courtesy of faithful fans willing to overlook Lewis's migratory patterns. The score clock high above the ring seems to flicker on and off in response, and I struggle to concentrate, as though a concussion grenade has been thrown in my direction. Banners and scarves and homemade signs are raised with English pride, and Union Jacks flap across the upper deck, matching the suit worn by Frank Maloney, Lewis's diminutive manager. He conducts a chorus of "You'll Never Walk Alone." A rousing rendition of "God Save the Queen" follows. The hairs on the back of my neck stand at attention.

Evander Holyfield relies upon God more than country. He enters to gospel music. He sings along to the song: "Praise and strength to the Lord!" His purple-and-white trunks are emblazoned with the legend "Phil 4:13," a reference to one of his favourite biblical verses. "I can do all things through Christ which strengtheneth me," it reads. The English fans pour down a rain of taunts. Holyfield smiles. He has faith in his Higher Power.

The two fighters meet at the centre of the ring. Lewis towers over his opponent. His red-and-gold trunks would be pants on most men; he looks down at Holyfield's bald head and smirks. Holyfield continues to pray. He looks serene. God has told him the third round will be his. He will not be let down.

The opening bell rings. The Britons sing and clap as Lewis presses his advantage. He opens with a combination and dodges a wild swing from Holyfield. The American dances but seems tentative. It's Lewis who advances. He connects with one left and then another. Holyfield counters with a solid left of his own, but he looks completely overmatched. He seems desperate and begins to wrestle. Holyfield lifts Lewis and almost flips him to the canvas as the round comes to a close. Both fighters are warned by the referee, Arthur Mercante, after the bell rings. Lewis spins away from the centre of the ring in disgust and returns to his corner.

Lewis continues to drive forward during the second round. He often treats boxing too much like chess, but he looks aggressive and sets the pace this time around. He lands a combination and two straight lefts and then presses Holyfield into the ropes for a series of punches. Lewis catches Holyfield's body several times and his head at least once. Damage has been done. Holyfield likely gives thanks when the bell rings. The English fans resume their chants during the break between rounds. One half of the arena claps and cries, "Lewis!" The other half echoes the challenge. The g continues until both sides are hoarse.

The third round — The Third Round — comes next. The American fans, who have been drowned out by the more vocal Britons, finally wake up. Holyfield does, too. He charges Lewis at the sound of the bell, bulldogging him into a corner. Holyfield throws three big punches, two rights and a left. Lewis looks stunned. He might be hurt. The fans at ringside stand in anticipation of a knockout. The English rowdies urge their hero to counter. Holyfield misses with an uppercut, but he lands another solid left. Lewis dances to safety and throws a barrage of defensive punches. He's on the run. But the final seconds of the round tick away before Holyfield's able to land a conclusive punch.

The Americans and Britons unite in cheers when the bell rings. It's been a frantic three minutes. I try to find traces of emotion through my binoculars. Lewis is overcome with relief when he finds his corner. Part of him must have feared that Holyfield's prediction would come true. Across the ring, Holyfield sits on his stool, looks down at his feet, and shakes his head. He looks as I imagine I did when Trevor Berbick beat Shane Sutcliffe. He might have won the round, but his prediction, his belief, has proven unfounded. The fight will last more than nine minutes. It will last far longer in Holyfield's soul. A sign in the crowd reads, "Like Monica, Evander's All Mouth." The confused look on Holyfield's face suggests the fight just might be all over, finished like his faith.

Yet the fourth round is calm. The frenzy of the third round wore out both fighters, who now seem happy to pace the ring. The referee urges Lewis and Holyfield to come together and box. (Mercante's order is the high-water mark of the frame.) Holyfield reluctantly backs Lewis into a corner, but nothing comes of it. Lewis appears content to coast.

But Lewis finds his energy once again in the fifth round. He moves well for a big man, and he manages to turn Holyfield toward the ring's edge. He begins to pick Holyfield apart. Lewis sets up Holyfield with a series of left jabs and follows through with overhand rights. The bombs land with cracks. Holyfield almost falls through the ropes. He tries to escape with a clash of heads, but Lewis keeps him at a safe distance. Lewis is in total command. He knows it. He finishes the round with several swivels of his hips. The dance reminds me of Berbick yet again, but the cheap seats respond with a roar of appreciation, not laughter.

Holyfield is upset at the display. He goes on the attack to open the sixth round. He lands a solid left hand. He combines it with a right. An exchange of wild punches follows. Lewis goes inside and lands an uppercut. Holyfield misses with a big right hand, and Lewis counters with a good right lead. But Lewis seems out of sorts. At the sound of blocks clapping — indicating that ten seconds remain in the round — Lewis turns away from Holyfield and walks toward his corner. The referee has to stop him. The round ends with Lewis bouncing about the ring. He stays out of harm's way, but Lewis has fresh marks around his eyes and nose. It's been a close, tough round. The fight's outcome is less clear. A low rumble, the murmur of debate, carries through the crowd.

Lewis tries to erase any doubts with a strong seventh round. He paws at Holyfield and pumps repeated jabs. Holyfield's head snaps back with disturbing regularity. It's all too easy. Lewis holds off a little during the eighth round, and Holyfield tries to capitalize on the opening. The pair exchange several punches in the centre of the ring. Few of the blows land for points. The round ends quietly. Lewis seems okay with letting Holyfield take the frame. He's grown soft again. Lewis is afraid that one punch will turn the fight around. He gives Holyfield too much respect.

Lewis continues to back off during the ninth round. Holyfield flashes a couple of jabs, and they might be enough to take an uneventful three minutes. The biggest fight in a decade is fast becoming a bore. But Lewis offers a hard finish to the frame. Holyfield's left eye begins to swell when he returns to his corner. His cut man presses a cold compress against the bruise and splashes water on Holyfield's steaming head, burning with the knowledge that he'll need a knockout to win.

Holyfield goes for the KO at the start of the tenth. He drives his head forward and hits Lewis in the jaw. Lewis stops to complain to the referee. Holyfield lands a couple of light punches while Lewis argues with Mercante. Lewis smiles in response. "Little man," he seems to say. The upper deck begins to shake with delight. Holyfield rallies with a combination and lands a punch to the body, but the referee separates the fighters when Lewis leans back on the ropes. Perhaps the last good chance for a knockout has been stolen.

But Lewis continues to rest too much. He chooses not to seal his victory. The eleventh round is devoid of action. I tell the reporter from the *Palm Beach Post* that Lewis will have to close with a flourish to guarantee a win. This is New York, after all: tourists always get taken in the Big Apple. Fortunately, Lewis comes through. He dominates Holyfield for the final three minutes. He scores at will. He takes big swings and earns points with solid punches. The English fans cheer wildly as the round and the fight conclude. The Americans are silent and remain in their seats. Lewis pumps his right fist in celebration. He will be crowned the heavy-weight champion of the world.

The ring fills with both camps. Holyfield stands in his corner. He looks dejected. He seems in a daze, still plagued by questions about the third round. Lewis is less contemplative. He is embraced by friends and well-wishers. Hugs all around. Lewis has made good on his promise. He'll walk out of the ring with all three belts, and his place in history will never again be insecure. The fight was far from spectacular, but it has been decisive. I look at my scorecard and tally the results. I have given the fight to Lewis, 116–113.

Tense minutes pass. The English fans continue to sing. A few Americans look for the exits. The bell rings. The announcer steps forward. His words serve to stun.

Eugenia Williams, an American judge, somehow scored the fight in favour of Holyfield, 115–113. Lewis crunches up his face: "What the fuck?" it reads. He looks at his corner in confusion. Holyfield, too, seems shocked. The announcer reads the score from the second judge, Stanley Christodoulou of South Africa. He gave the fight to Lewis, 116–113. Lewis nods in agreement. I nod with him, pleased by the validation. All will be right. There is one score yet to be announced, but the third judge is an Englishman named Larry O'Connell. He almost certainly has scored the fight for Lewis.

It's not to be. O'Connell scored the bout even, 115–115. The fight is declared a draw. Both fighters retain their respective titles. Neither is declared the unified champion.

There's a moment, less than a single second, when the entire arena grows quiet. Then the American fans rise to their feet and cry out with joy. The Britons either stand in disbelief or quake with anger. I'm too surprised to be scared. An English hood stands in the middle of the aisle in front of me and challenges any American in the audience to a fight. "Tell me Holyfield won and I'll smash your fucking face!" he threatens. Other men rush up to the press section and plead, "Just write the truth. Please tell the world the truth." It's as though we're reporting on genocide. But we haven't witnessed murder, only robbery.

I scramble to pack my bags. I return my rented binoculars, run toward the arena basement via a staff stairway, scream at a security guard to let me in, elbow my way to the media centre, and lift the final fight statistics from a fellow reporter. The numbers provide a compelling argument on behalf of Lewis. (The statistics even make me doubt my relatively narrow margin of victory.) Lewis landed 348 punches compared to 130 for Holyfield. Lewis connected with 187 jabs; Holyfield found the mark with only 52. Lewis landed 161 power punches; Holyfield countered with only 78 of his own. In six of the rounds, Holyfield landed fewer than ten punches. He had been invisible for fully half of the fight.

Photocopies of the official scorecards are passed from hand to hand. They leave our mouths open wide and our eyes asking questions. Eugenia Williams awarded Holyfield seven rounds — including the fifth, when Lewis had Holyfield on the ropes and outlanded him 43–11. Remarkably, Larry O'Connell also had Lewis behind heading into the final round. Had Lewis not won the frame in convincing fashion, he would have lost the fight in a majority decision. A draw was bad enough. Defeat would have been a catastrophe.

There is no appeal process in boxing, yet I can't help thinking the decision will be overturned. There has to be some way to settle the score. Boxing is legendary for its corruption, its population of bad men on greased wheels. But millions of people watched Lennox Lewis beat Evander Holyfield. The newspaper headlines will scream, "Fix!" The heavyweight championship will be declared a sham. Boxing's lost glory was to be regained tonight in New York. The sport has been floored instead.

I'm upset more than anything else. After the Trevor Berbick drama, I don't want to write that boxing deserves to be in dire straits. And I don't want to write about greed and bagmen and secret signals. I want to write about the spectacle. I want to write about the noise. I want to write about the celebration.

Pure and simple, I want to write about a fight. Unfortunately, the fight is the only thing that doesn't seem to matter.

SUNDAY

It's early Sunday morning when the post-fight press conference is set to begin. It's not a happy room. There are not enough seats, and several people have to sit on the floor or crouch down in the aisles. The cameramen who line the back wall bawl at reporters when they lift their heads in the way. A few skirmishes break out as rumours of a fix quickly circulate. I can find only two writers who gave the fight to Holyfield, and they don't defend their scores adamantly. Most of the writers share another opinion: we have witnessed boxing's lowest point, at least for this month.

The room continues to simmer when the proceedings are delayed. A dark mood settles over the place. Tensions rise higher still when Lewis finally appears with his mother, Violet; his trainer, Emanuel Steward; and his manager, Frank Maloney. They are united in rage. Holyfield arrives next, accompanied by his trainer, Don Turner, and the felonious Don King. The Warrior looks battered. His face is swollen, and he holds an ice pack to his stomach beneath a loose purple top. He says he's only catching cramps, but he looks like a man who knows loss. Both Lewis and Holyfield appear exhausted. Their faces — puffy, eyes unblinking — also carry a fair amount of shock. Only King, who beams brightly when he takes to the stage, is not at a loss for words. He stands to make a great deal of money from a rematch.

"We had a great promotion and a great fight," King begins. "Judging is subjective. A significant thing is the Brit. One of his fellow countrymen is the one who made the call. Who am I to be second-guessing the judges? They rendered the decision. They did the best they could. What do you do when you have a dispute? You resolve it. Let's do it again." Whispers of disgust greet King's proposal. I have to stop myself from walking out.

"This is great," he continues, undaunted. "I love this. There's going to be a tomorrow! There's going to be a tomorrow!" King sounds like a preacher who has found God for a second time, unable to contain his joy. "What a wonderful night!" he roars. "Hear my cry: V-I-C-T-O-R-Y!" His smile is the only one in the room.

Lewis is understandably livid. "I cannot believe the outcome," he says. "It was my time to shine and they ripped me off. They ripped me off. I am the undisputed heavyweight champion, and the whole world knows that. Evander should give me those two belts because he knows they're mine." Lewis's mother goes face to face with Holyfield. She wants him to admit that he's lost. Holyfield waves her away with a dismissive flap of his hand. Lewis expresses his displeasure with the gesture. It looks as though the two fighters might get busy again. No cool heads remain to prevail.

Holyfield looks meek after the dust has settled. He tries to convince reporters that he won the fight, but the boasts come off as hollow. "I feel like a champion," Holyfield says. "I can't fight and score. People at ringside are not the judges." He exhales with the despair of a drowning man whose life ring is well out of reach. The doubt will soon break him. Later he'll plead that he was sick prior to the fight. His stomach and legs cramped up, and he very nearly didn't enter the ring. Holyfield will never admit that he lost the fight straight up, but the confession betrays his heart. How often do winners make excuses?

It's Emanuel Steward who has the evening's last word. His hands shake when he snatches the microphone from the table. He provides a fitting conclusion to a sorry display. "It wasn't even close," he steams. "It was a total mismatch. Holyfield couldn't even be his sparring partner. This," he says, "this is what's killing boxing." Feedback echoes through the room when Steward tosses away the microphone. He and Lewis storm back to their locker room together. The press conference breaks up.

I decide to chase after Frank Maloney. He's usually good for a quote, and his anger might push him to say something even more outlandish than usual. Moving through the crowd is like trying to run through deep water, but I somehow find myself pressed against Maloney in the middle of a massive scrum. He's only as tall as my shoulder. But for a small man he's known to pack a punch. He doesn't let me down.

He calls the judges "Stevie Wonder, Ray Charles, and some other blind person." I can't help laughing. He's encouraged by the response. He collapses into a rant that steadily picks up speed. "For boxing's sake," he says, "there has to be a rematch. But forget about the titles. Throw the titles in the bin. Ten years of hard work, and we got robbed. I'm in shock." He pauses. I know he's about to spill wide open. "Maybe Don King paid someone off," Maloney finally says. I can feel the scrum buckle. "I'm saying it. It's funny that O'Connell got the job within two weeks of doing the De La Hoya–Quartey fight. It's never happened before. You don't expect that from a British judge, do you?" Maloney adds that he'll file an official complaint.

I need a response from Don King to complete the story. It will prove difficult to reach him. He has plunked himself down on a chair on the distant stage, where he sits like Buddha in a fright wig. I push my way out of the Maloney scrum, wade through several other huddles, and emerge next to King. He turns to me and smiles. Other reporters crowd around. I'm nervous. I'm about to confront boxing's most powerful promoter with allegations that he fixed a fight, and I'm not quite sure how to begin.

"Mr. King, I'm sorry to ask you this question," I say, "but Frank Maloney suggested that you may have paid off one of the judges. He also suggested —"

"Oh, come on. I'm not even going to dignify that —"

"He said official complaints will be filed —"

"He can do whatever he has to do. Whatever he has to do. I welcome it."

"So you have no response?"

"I have no response to that. I won't even dignify that. You're a handsome young man, too, you know what I mean? Such courage. You're a handsome guy. You've got your whole life ahead of you. You're going to be a brilliant reporter."

"Do you two want to be alone?" cracks a New York writer standing nearby.

"No!" I say a little too quickly, wondering whether King knows me from Adam.

I turn again to King: "You've got no further comment on that?"

"What do you want me to say?" he asks. He pauses for a moment. His eyes shift back and forth. He completes an unseen calculation. "You felt shame asking that question, didn't you?" he demands. "You were embarrassed to bring that type of a message."

"I felt like a tattle-tale," I say. An honest reply. The other reporters laugh.

"That answers it for me. I mean, it's so unlike you. You have such integrity, such honour. I can't believe you . . . some of the old veterans, yes, but a youngster? To be contaminated like that? To be contaminated with a cancer? I don't believe it."

I get defensive. "But I had to tell you what he said."

"I know," King replies. "You did that. Tell him I love him."

A woman with a microphone interjects. "Yes, I am from Polish television," she says. "Do you think there is any chance Holyfield will go up against Lewis in the United Kingdom?" Lewis has already insisted that any rematch be held on English soil.

King's face explodes with a smile. "I love the Poles," he begins. "The Polish people really touch my heart. They are fighters. They believe in fighting for their rights. I shall not ever forget, when the blitzkrieg was there, and Hitler was running through Poland, the people had to resist him. They fought back, not having the mechanized Panzer that Hitler had, but they had the heart, the courage, the intestinal fortitude, to continue to reject oppression and tyranny. And so, I love the Polish people, and I would love to be anywhere, do anything, that would be motivating and inspiring to those great people. I love you all."

Don King has worked his magic. Truth has no hold on his tongue. But he makes people feel good about themselves. In the space of two minutes he had me convinced that I was handsome and left the Poles on top of the world. And so, again and again, he is forgiven — though maybe not this time.

It's well past 2 a.m. when all has been said and nothing is done. I walk back to the Chelsea, my head spinning with the night's events. It's been an unbelievable evening. I still can't fathom what has taken place. I unlock my door and wonder where I'll find myself come morning.

I throw down my bag and turn on my computer. Its familiar blue glow fills my room. I write until the sun begins to filter through the shutters and outshines the screen. I sit back and re-read my work by first light. I make it plain that Lewis was taken. It sounds so over-the-top that the firmness of my stance leaves me unsure of myself. Despite all the evidence, I'm not certain I'm on the right side of the debate, and I want a second opinion, advice by newsprint proxy. I go outside to buy the New York papers that have already hit the streets and stop by Krispy Kreme for a fill-up. I return to my room, spread the papers out on my bed, tuck into a bag of donuts, and begin to read. All the writers — including Michael Katz and Wally Matthews, the biggest of the big — have favoured Lewis by a wide margin. Enormous headlines declare the decision was unjust at best, criminal at worst. I smile inside, feeling good about what I've written. I plug my computer into the phone line and file. My editor confirms that the story has landed. My work in New York is done. I allow myself to fall into a deep sleep.

I wake up later in the afternoon with a start. My television has turned itself on. The beast has a mind of its own. I flick to a sports channel. The fight is the talk of the day. The judges are held up as villains. They'll face intense scrutiny over the coming days.

Larry O'Connell will eventually apologize for his poor scoring. He'll say he believed Lewis won the fight, and that he felt sick when his scorecard came out a tie. He thought there must have been an error in addition. There hadn't been, but simple mathematics provide a convenient excuse. His conscience cleared, O'Connell will disappear into obscurity.

Eugenia Williams will not escape so easily. It's revealed that she declared bankruptcy shortly before the fight, and there are suspicions that a large lump sum was deposited into one of her bank accounts. She will later be called to testify at state and federal investigations into the fight. The official inquiries will amount to

★★ JUDGE EUGENIA WILLIAMS ENDURES HER OBSTRUCTED VIEW OF LENNOX LEWIS HAMMERING EVANDER HOLYFIELD

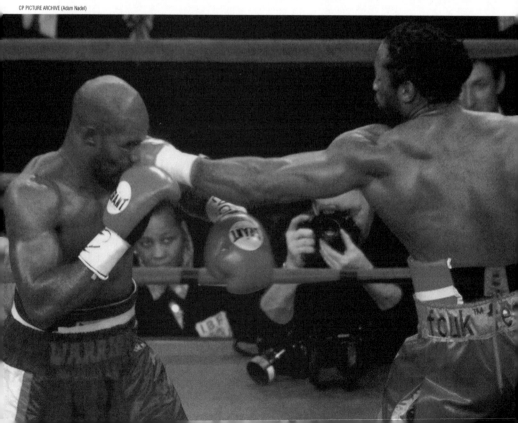

nothing — they are widely dismissed as political posturing during an election year — but Williams will endure some pointed questioning. Her answers are feeble for the most part. Williams argues that she couldn't see Lewis hit Holyfield during much of the fight because she didn't have a good view of the action. "I scored what blows I could actually see," she pleads. "When I got a clear view, I scored the blows that I actually saw." Replays show Williams seated next to the apron. At no time was her view obstructed. But she remains steadfast, much to the delight of late-night television comedians. Williams will never be sanctioned for her part in the Holyfield-Lewis scandal, but she won't work another fight.

Only Stanley Christodoulou, the South African judge who favoured Lewis, will be left unmolested. He later condemns his fellow judges. "I must be frank with you," he tells a television reporter. "I didn't think it was that difficult. From the outset, Mr. Lewis dominated the fight. I think that the time has come to re-evaluate the system. They should appoint three neutral judges." Christodoulou's comments will serve to intensify the attacks on Williams and O'Connell, but little of substance will come of them. Boxing will experiment with open scoring for a short time, but it is never widely implemented. Officials are satisfied with the status quo.

Even as my room fills with sunlight, I know boxing will never change. It has always been rotten. Dirty. Suspect. I've been part of the game for exactly four fights, and I can count a long list of acquaintances hard done by: Otis Grant, Mike Tyson, Muhammad Ali, Shane Sutcliffe, Trevor Berbick. And now Lennox Lewis. There's no way he'll be the last.

A touch of NYC bravado is burned into me with the heat of the afternoon. On my first day in town, an elderly man jumped from the top of a Manhattan skyscraper. He hit a female pedestrian before he hit the pavement. She was on her lunch hour. The old man burst open when he hit the woman; he disintegrated when he struck the sidewalk.

The woman was left with a broken arm and soaked in someone

else's blood. The old man was scraped clean of the cement and shovelled into plastic bags.

And outside that section of liquid sidewalk, Gotham's life continued apace.

Boxing's routine will go on, too. With or without Lennox Lewis, with or without me. New fights, hyped as the best of the year, the decade, even the century, will be staged. Young fighters will work their way out of clubs. Old fighters will live off tarnished trophies. And yellow-eyed reporters will continue to watch the unfolding drama, express rage when it's called for, ecstasy on those rare occasions when boxing lives up to its billing. Fuck it, I figure. I may as well join in. Hitch on the night train for the long haul.

I'll sweep into exotic towns, eat free food and down free alcohol, watch a fight or two, and try to profit from it. Why not? The pain I'll leave to the fighters. I won't get involved beyond my honey-glazed dispatches. Boxing's parade of losers will be welcomed through my life's revolving door. Tell me their sad stories so I can file them and forget them.

★ **5** ★

THE ILLUSTRATED BOXER

★ STÉPHANE OUELLET V. DAVEY HILTON JR. ★

MAY 28, 1999

"I'm going to take this right foot, and I'm going to whomp you on that side of your face."

— ACTOR TOM LAUGHLIN IN *BILLY JACK*

STABLE

Davey Hilton Jr. and Stéphane Ouellet. Two more boxers I'll bleed dry. They are set to meet Friday night at the Molson Centre in Montreal, my first fight since going cold in New York. I'm ready for anything. The train ride northeast gives me time to prepare for another letdown. Another meltdown.

But this night might be memorable, I can hear my old self say. It promises to be the biggest Canadian prizefight in history — if not in the ring, then at least in combined purse. And on the surface of things, the pairing looks to have everything going for it.

The two men regard each other with deep hatred. They first fought the previous November, three days before the heated Quebec provincial election. Hilton, the *maudit anglais*, came from behind to win a bloody contest in the twelfth and final round. Both boxers had just engaged in the most important fight of their lives, and it had been an electric evening, every moment a snapshot. The bitter rivalry was made permanent in the annals of Canadian boxing legend.

Fights between English and French boxers have always played well in Montreal. (Hilton fought two popular bouts with Mario Cusson in the 1980s.) Only the Canadian middleweight title was at stake when Hilton and Ouellet first met, but 18,000 fans had been in attendance. More than 20,000 are expected to pack into the Molson Centre for the Battle of Quebec, Part Deux. It doesn't hurt that the championship belt is only part of the deal. Ouellet has come close to retirement several times since his painful loss to Hilton. The promotion looked to be in even greater jeopardy when Hilton was charged with the sexual assault of two young girls just weeks before the fight. But Hilton got out on bail, and Ouellet decided to go out for revenge. There will be no ill-bred hearts in the ring, we're told. It will be a desperate clash. "It is impossible for this to be a lousy fight," says Yvon Michel, a representative of promoter InterBox, which dubbed the rematch "The Ultimate Verdict." Perhaps reality will finally exceed expectation. I look forward to the fight, if only because there's an outside shot it will give me reason to care.

After checking into my hotel, I make my way to the Centre Claude Robillard in the city's north end. It's a bunker of a building, brutal and low to the ground, but the home to training facilities for a museum-worthy collection of sports. There are swimming pools, dojos, gymnastics studios, and archery galleries. The needs of boxers are also met. Down in the basement, accessible through hallways thick with the smell of chlorine and sweat, a corner has been set aside for the making of fighters. It's protected from outside interference by white mosquito nets. Two rings occupy much of the floor space, but there is room for leather-wrapped heavy bags, speed bags, and the jumping of ropes. The walls are covered with posters and stained mirrors. A small stereo crackles. It's not luxurious, but all the fighters in InterBox's stable work out here. It's a clubhouse that requires no guard dog.

I poke my head through the mosquito nets. I want to watch Ouellet train, but he doesn't appear to be in attendance. I ask one of the coaches present about Ouellet's schedule. He says, "Be patient." He points toward a stack of metal chairs that sit in front of a bank of lockers at one end of the room. I make myself comfortable.

Four boxers — I recognize only Dale Brown, a bruising Canadian cruiserweight prone to cuts — are in the midst of their routines. Brown is dressed in a tight track suit. He has the hood of his sweatshirt pulled up. He boxes with his shadow for several rounds. I watch as his face becomes wet and stains grow on his chest and in his armpits. He skids across the floor, the bottoms of his feet hitting the ground lightly each time he throws a fist at a phantom target. He isn't terribly graceful. I'm sure he would like to move more smoothly. But he does his best to bob and weave, and I enjoy the display, feel myself being drawn in. Brown demonstrates a deep desire to improve. I'm struck by his attention to detail, to craft, and the performance gives me pause. Despite the number of black eyes I've already witnessed in boxing, at the heart of the sport is a drive toward betterment. A boxer works to perfect his jab, which makes him a more dangerous fighter, which makes him a possible contender, which makes him a potential champion, which makes him an exception to the rule that a hard-knock kid must end his life in the gutter. Brown has flaws — the scars on his temples prove as much — but he fights to overcome them. He wants a shot at The Show, and he has hope that his time will be at hand. He need only work: the sweat that makes his clothes heavy will make the rest of his load lighter.

I snap my mind back to reality before the strings come in with the aid of a tough-looking newcomer. He has a prominent brow and a head of spiked hair that he keeps long at the back, a classic mullet. He makes his way slowly across the room and faces the mirror that occupies the wall most distant from me. None of the other fighters takes notice when the man begins to strip down. He takes off each item of clothing with cool intent, and when he removes another garment and drops it to the floor, he steps back and examines his body in the mirror. After several minutes he stares at a reflection clad only in white briefs. He's slender and well proportioned. His skin is deeply tanned and laden with tattoos. He guides his rough hands across his shoulders and down the opposite arm before rubbing his belly and chest. His breathing becomes more purposeful as he explores his form. At last he takes another step away from the mirror and watches as his body becomes taut. Each muscle looks ready for action, but the man stays perfectly still. He appears about to enter a trance.

His eyes finally blink once, then twice. He puts his clothes back on. He begins to wrap his hands. He's ready. He has assured himself that he's prepared for a fight. I am impressed by his quiet meditation, the restoration of his faith in himself.

INK

The boxer in the mirror is Stéphane Ouellet. Unlike most artists, he first used himself as a canvas: his skin bears not only boxing's scars, but also that impressive collection of tattoos. There is the crucifix that spikes his stomach, held in place by a chain that wraps around his neck. The image of Jesus Christ has been etched into his left forearm. An intricate Celtic design combines to form a point on the top of his left hand, aimed at his third knuckle. Two martini glasses are engraved into his left biceps. The names of his two young sons, Jim and William, have earned a place on his body. The names of his parents, Olivette and Ange-Émile, decorate Ouellet's right arm. An inkwell and a feather are carved into his left arm. A rose graces his right biceps, and strung-up boxing gloves occupy the skin over his heart.

Each illustration — uniformly rendered in green ink — gives a clue to his character, a hint of understanding. But when taken as a whole, his torso's tapestry provides a more complete narrative, a rebel's contradictory tale. It will be a challenge to create a just portrait. Ouellet is a hero in Quebec, an unknown in the proverbial Rest of Canada, a deep thinker in a sport of thugs, a man with bad friends and good children: a Fighting Poet. His rematch with Davey Hilton Jr. is the latest chapter in an already compelling story — though their first fight almost closed the book.

"That fight," Ouellet says after his workout, "I thought about quitting after that fight. It was so hard. And I was so embarrassed. I felt like I had let down my fans. I wasn't sure I could face them again." He shifts in his chair and looks over at Yvon Michel, who has joined us. Even talking about the night makes him uncomfortable. It's still too close to the bone.

It was the previous November. Ouellet was on a roll. He was set for a world-title match against Hacine Cherifi. "I was looking ahead," he admits. But now he's forced to look back. At the moment he lost his shot at Cherifi. The instant he lost his will to go on.

"He had the attitude that boxing was a hobby then," says Michel, who had trained Ouellet for the fight. "He didn't prepare like it was a championship fight. He trained like it was a hobby, like it was for fun."

It was not. Ouellet was twenty-seven years old when he met Hilton, who was eight hard years his senior. The younger boxer built a substantial lead on points during the early rounds, outpacing Hilton, an out-of-shape alcoholic. But Hilton broke Ouellet's nose in the third round. Blood poured into his mouth from a place deep inside his head, a hot spring of iron and salt. The guard that capped his teeth was repeatedly washed out of his mouth. Each time it fell to the canvas, Ouellet bent over to pick it up, like a drunk fumbling for his keys. But he couldn't attend to his lungs so easily. He fought for nine rounds without oxygen, unable to breathe through his shattered nose or blood-filled mouth. He was dazed and exhausted when Hilton pressed him against the ropes in the final round. The referee stopped the fight. Hilton bounced up and down in celebration, embraced by his family. Ouellet looked relieved, glad it was over.

"But when he woke up the next day," says Michel, bringing us back to the present, "he hurt. He really took Hilton lightly last time. And he said if he lost against him, that was it." Ouellet began to contemplate retirement, began to think about a second career. "I didn't want to do boxing anymore," he says. "I decided I was a failure. A loser."

Only hours of consultation with his Higher Power convinced him otherwise. "If I didn't have a lot of faith in God," Ouellet says, "I would be finished. I wouldn't be here right now." He sounds genuine to me, not at all like the football players who thank the Lord Jesus Christ for touchdowns. "He got me through it," he says. "Thank God." Even strong men need to call on outside help sometimes, and Ouellet's faith rings true. I don't feel the least bit cynical. A miracle in itself.

"Hilton gave him a lot of maturity," says Michel, moving along the conversation like a conductor invisibly calling for more trumpet. "He has pushed very hard every day. He's suffering in training so he does not suffer in the ring."

Training does not come easily to Ouellet. The tattoos suggest he harbours no love for authority, for conformity. "I don't like to be told what to do," he says. "And I don't like to run just to run." He has a strange relationship with boxing. Most fighters are seduced by the sport, slip into things like I have. Then they find it hard to leave when the end comes, lingering on the platform. I get a different sense from Ouellet. Part of him might even hate boxing, the way a child hates a chore.

"I never loved boxing," he confirms when asked about his introduction to the sport. "I was only an excuse. My sister was in love with a fighter. She wanted me to go to the gym so she could watch him." But the young tough, a loner who roamed the streets of his hometown of Jonquière, showed immediate potential. "A natural," says Michel.

Yet because he was naturally talented — and because he took to regimen like a duck to an oven — he never felt the need to train. "He was so hard to control," remembers Michel. "It cost him." Ouellet didn't have the discipline to fight on the Olympic team, and he pissed away his six amateur titles on hard living and bad company.

He fell in with the Hells Angels, and legions of bikers showed up at his fights after he turned pro in 1991. Mainstream appeal did not fit inside motorcycle leathers. Especially in gang-wartorn Montreal, the bikers added a sense of doom to Ouellet's fights. Something frightening. All boxers are dangerous men, but there's a very black patch inside Ouellet. I'm just having trouble finding it. The ink on his skin acts like a shield.

"My children," he says suddenly of his two boys, further hampering my efforts, "they are very important to me. When you put your children on Earth, you want to give your children the best. They helped me, too." His first fight with Davey Hilton's brother Alex — whom he knocked out twice, adding to the bad blood between the families — was delayed by a stint in rehab. But because he wanted to do right by his sons, he quit drinking, diverted the energies he poured into his social life into fatherhood instead. "I spend as much time as I can with them," says Ouellet. "They keep me honest. I try my best."

Ouellet's own parents must have been surprised by the son they produced. His father paints and his mother runs an art gallery. A boxer seemed an unlikely offspring. "Hilton was raised to be a fighter," Michel says. "He is from a family of traditionalists. Stéphane is not." But the influence of his parents was not lost on Ouellet. He took from them an artist's pretension. "He's a good boxer, obviously," says Michel. "But he has more of an artistic intent than an athletic intent." I smile at the lame try for diplomacy, Michel's gentle way of saying Ouellet lacks focus. To keep Ouellet's mind (and body) from wandering before the rematch, Michel took his pupil to Puerto Rico for a camp made secure by isolation. "He couldn't go anywhere, so he ran on the spot," Michel laughs.

An end was also put to Ouellet's chief distraction from the ring post-rehab: poetry. His written work was not lighthearted stuff. Sex and death. Suicide and alcohol. While the introspection earned him fans, he has given up the ghost before he confronts that of Hilton. "That's finished," he says. "When you are a boxer, you think all that you do is good. There is ego. I have read a lot since, and my humility saved me. I've seen children who write better poetry than me.

"No more."

Ouellet will soon say as much about boxing. "I don't want to do this forever," he says. He will earn enough to provide for his family, and then there's a childhood dream he wants to fulfil. "What's that?" I ask. Ouellet searches for the proper term *en anglais*, consults with Michel, and they agree on the word. "I want to be an embalmer," he says. "Is that how you say it?" The three of us chuckle at the prospect. "Oh, come on!" says Michel. "They are not that different, boxing and embalming. He likes to bury people. It's fitting."

We laugh again before Ouellet ends the session on a serious note. "I love the fight," he whispers. "The stress, the risk, the adrenaline. I love the mystique that surrounds boxing. People want a show, and I give a show. It's very hard to control the pressure, to control the stress. Once you are in the ring, you must control it — with your power. This power gives you victory."

HILTON AT THE PLAZA

I don't get the chance to examine Davey Hilton's psyche as closely, but I have a good idea that his head has no space reserved for philosophy. His family, the Famous Fighting Hiltons, is not the sort to concern itself with art or poetry. Instead, all five Hilton boys — Davey is the eldest — busied themselves with punch-ups under their father's glassy eye. Only Matthew Hilton started high school. He was probably the most talented of the bunch as a boxer, but he inherited his dad's love of the bottle, got fat, and was rendered too damaged to compete.

The other boys also have their tales of woe. Stewart Hilton was killed in a car accident in 1986. Alex Hilton has served time for assault; his prison sentence was extended when he supervised the gang rape of a convicted child molester while behind bars. Even Davey Hilton Sr., the aging patriarch, lives up to his clan's black reputation. A few months before his son fought Ouellet for the first time, the senior Hilton took exception to a sixty-three-year-old man in a LaSalle Wal-Mart and knocked him out. Watch for falling geezers.

But Davey Hilton Jr. has the most colourful past. He is blessed with significant power despite his relatively compact stature. He enjoyed a solid start to his career, but his best shot at a world title — which came after he beat Dennis Horne in 1985 — slipped away when he wrecked his motorcycle. In the years since, he's fought sporadically and has broken the law almost as frequently. He was first locked away for drunk driving and assault. A more serious indiscretion came in 1991, when Matthew and Davey concocted an alcohol-fuelled plan to hold up a West Island Dunkin' Donuts at gunpoint. (They were instantly recognized and picked up by police within minutes.) Now he faces accusations that he repeatedly molested two girls between 1995 and 1998. Both victims were minors when the assaults — described by detectives as sexual interference and sexual touching — are alleged to have occurred. Not surprisingly, Hilton denies the most recent charges. But he cannot deny that he has lived a far from model existence.

Hence my discomfort when I run into Hilton in the elevator of the Maritime Plaza, a downtown hotel with a clam-shaped restaurant that will serve as my home base for the fight. He seems to sense that my nerves are on edge. He eyes me suspiciously. The elevator creeps up, inching toward my floor. Hilton continues to burrow into me with his glare. The elevator doors finally open. I step into the hallway. To my horror, Hilton exits with me. I brace myself for a blow to the back of the head. But Hilton tugs his room key, not a blackjack, free of his pocket. He unlocks the door immediately adjacent to mine. We will be neighbours for the week. I feel my stomach twist into itself.

I call Graham, my editor, immediately. "Davey Hilton's in the room right next to me," I hiss. "I'm scared shitless." Graham expresses no small amount of delight at my predicament. "Isn't that funny," he says. "Not really," I whisper, panicked. I read Graham a telling quotation from Hilton that followed his win over Ouellet: "Thank God the ref stepped in," Hilton had said. "He was defenceless. His hands were down. I wouldn't have stopped punching, and that's the time a guy can have brain damage. I'm no gentleman in the ring. That might have ended his life." Laughter on the other end of the line. "Sleep well," Graham says cheerfully before hanging up. I resolve to act with the discretion of a mouse in a cat-filled house. I'll spend as little time as possible in my room. When I have no choice but to return, I will avoid Hilton at all costs.

My plan is foiled later that same evening, after dinner. I walk a few blocks along a busy downtown street before stepping inside a magazine shop. I find my way to the back of the store, where the sports periodicals are shelved. It's too late to turn around when I notice Hilton. He's killing time. He flips through a fistful of boxing magazines, perhaps looking for his name or predictions for his fight with Ouellet. Another distraction awaits. A box containing a new stereo pokes out of a plastic bag at his feet.

But first he attends to me. He looks up from his magazines and sees me staring wide-eyed back at him. His face crinkles with a hint of recognition. I hope he doesn't think I'm stalking him. We continue to look at each other as his mind ticks off possible connections. He finally decides I'm harmless and nods. I offer a weak smile in return and exhale. My continued exposure to dangerous men has left me wired. The anxiety is ill-founded in one sense: why would world-class boxers waste their time on me? Yet my fears also have a logical foundation, given the badness to which I've been privy.

I am still determined not to part with boxing. But like a pregnant woman who can't stop smoking, I hope my vice will not sting me. I'd better my odds of survival, I decide, were I not within striking distance of Hilton. I grab a random magazine, pay, and head for the door.

THE ULTIMATE VERDICT

The pipe and drum band that will escort Davey Hilton Jr. to the ring waits next to the press room in the bowels of the Molson Centre. The kilted troops are proud supporters of Montreal's RCAF Association (306 Wing) and have long been linked with the Hilton clan. "We're Davey's good luck charm," one of the drummers yells above the muffled din of the crowd. "We can't be beat." A French reporter betrays his allegiance when he responds to the boast: "We'll see about that."

The big crowd makes its feelings equally plain. The arena is virtually sold out, and just about every person in attendance seems to favour Ouellet. Even though his customary army of Hells Angels is largely absent — the result of a dispute between the bikers and the promoter — he still enjoys the majority of the support. As the undercard progresses, the pre-fight preparations for Hilton and Ouellet flash on the octagonal score clock that hangs above the ring. The crowd roars whenever the French Canadian's tattoos and taped hands appear. Hilton's image is accompanied by a chorus of loud jeers. The invective surely carries into his dressing room, but Hilton pushes away the sound, smiles, winks, and flashes a victory sign. His defiance makes the crowd more surly. Montrealers have always had a hearty appetite for destruction.

The night seems to unfold in slow motion prior to the Main Event. The undercard is decent — Dale Brown wins his bout — but not enough to quench the building's bloodlust. The early fights are dismissed by most of those present as mere clutter. Only Hilton v. Ouellet, only Anglo v. Franco, only Thug v. Poet appear to matter. Foreplay is ignored in favour of the climax.

The cameras of the American television network ESPN2 are readied. High-strung technicians create an ever-growing pile of cigarette ends on the concrete floor at ringside. The Molson Centre is increasingly transformed into a sonic beacon with each pulse of energy. I can't help feeling a sense of anticipation that has been foreign to me since Otis Grant faced Roy Jones Jr. I can't wait to punch the clock.

Ouellet, in the unfamiliar role of challenger, begins his long walk to the ring. Cameras record his travels from the dressing room and beam the signals to the anxious crowd via the score clock. He picks his way through an endless series of tunnels before he appears on the arena floor. A spotlight then tracks his journey. The glare flashes off his gold trunks and the black satin uniforms of his corner. A sweeping work by Vangelis fills the air with song. The imposing music fuels both Ouellet's courage and the fury of his fans. Sanity is the evening's first casualty. My head feels as though it's just gone through a windshield.

Ouellet climbs through the ropes and awaits his opponent. Hilton, dressed in a white robe decorated with the Scottish lion, begins his own march toward the canvas. Incredible emotion erupts when his battalion reaches the floor. From my vantage point at ringside, I can see the tops of the pipes as the air force band, awash in bright light, makes its way slowly through the crowd. But the corps is rendered mute by the wall of noise created by the fans. I can hear only the pounding of the bass drum — or perhaps I feel it, deep within my guts. When the procession reaches the ring, I see that Alex Hilton has led the charge. He holds his brother's belt, the same one that had belonged to Ouellet, high in the air. Alex stares at the man who has twice rendered him unconscious and mouths: "The champ, the champ, the champ." Ouellet looks down at his feet with a mixture of shame and trepidation.

"In the red corner," the ring announcer begins. That's all I hear before the crowd drowns out the introductions. It's as though the announcer's microphone has been turned off. An intense staredown follows. It makes clear the hatred the boxers share. The roof rises a little bit more. After drama's necessary delay, the opening bell rings. Only then do I realize that I've been on my feet the entire time. Awakened by the sound of the bell, I quickly take to my seat and prepare to take notes, my pen shaking in my hand.

Hilton opens the fight on the offensive. He catches Ouellet squarely with his powerful left jab more than once. Ouellet looks tentative, perhaps even scared, though he could be conserving his strength in anticipation of a long fight. Hilton misses with a vicious left hook and misses his chance at a short night at the same time. Ouellet is jolted into action by the near blow. He scores some points when he responds with a flurry of late punches, but it's Hilton who dominates the round. The final seconds tick away. The bell rings. "That's it, boy," Hilton says to himself with a nod. "Fight your fight." His father gently provides grease to his face and offers advice during the break: "Stick with the jab!" he yells. Hilton listens.

The start of the second frame sees Hilton pump his left arm like the pistons of a muscle car. He launches five or six strikes in a row, takes a break, and fires another half-dozen blows. But Ouellet, who begins to look more comfortable, is able to counter his opponent's challenge. He takes his time with Hilton and manages to find open flesh to mark. It's a case of power versus precision, of heart versus head. Ouellet's more conservative tactics prove superior. He takes the second round with a convincing display of talent. The tight battle expected by all in attendance has commenced.

A surprise predicted by few will finish it. Hilton again goes on the attack in the third round. He overwhelms Ouellet and pushes him about the ring with relative ease. Hilton bullies him into corners and hurts Ouellet with several hard shots. In the round's final minute, Hilton lands a devastating left to the head of Ouellet, who staggers toward his corner. Hilton throws another left. Then a right. Both punches connect. Ouellet starts to fall toward the ropes without resistance. Hilton misses with another left, but he lands a second right. It's a brutal combination. Ouellet falls on his back and begins to sink into the canvas.

Ouellet does his best to rise. He takes to his feet and tries to focus on the referee waving his hands in front of his face. But he can't. At 2:48 of the third round, the fight is over. The crowd thunders. Its hero has been defeated. But the evening has still been worth the money.

There is cause for celebration — for Hilton especially. He begins to leap about the ring with his right fist raised. Alex Hilton lifts his brother to his shoulders and yells in triumph. Flowers are passed through the ropes.

The arena is cleared. The fighters return to their dressing rooms and take time to collect their disparate thoughts. The reporters adjourn to the press room and we begin to tap out stories. The start of the post-fight press conference, in an adjacent room, soon interrupts us. The dissection will have to wait.

Hilton enters with his father by his side. His mother, Jean, enters a little later. The Hiltons look like a perfect family in every way. Davey Hilton Jr. is at his charismatic best. He shakes hands. He gives thanks. He is respectful and polite. He appears deceptively benign. Only on rare occasion does a fighter's arrogance shine from his eyes. He knows his performance will see him move up through

★★★ **STÉPHANE OUELLET LOOKS STUNNED FOLLOWING A WET KISS FROM ARCH-ENEMY DAVEY HILTON JR.** ★★★

boxing's ranks and into position for a title shot. He talks about being part of a big-time fight against a million-dollar adversary. "I believe in comebacks," he says with conviction. "Before I quit, I'd like to fight the best. I've got nothing to lose. I know if I hit someone on the chin, he's going down. I don't care who it is." Belief washes over the observers in attendance. Perhaps the one-time contender will find redemption.

Only Hilton's dark past — and uncertain future — cast a shadow across the festivities. He faces a fourteen-year prison sentence if he's convicted of the two sexual assaults. At the very least, he won't be allowed to leave the province until the matter is settled. The court fight could take years. He could be separated from stardom by a border made concrete through crime. But his troubles go unmentioned. It's Ouellet who has to endure the more rigorous assault from reporters. His own hopes for a world-title shot are now entirely dashed, and the knowledge has settled deep within him. He spends much of the press conference with his head bowed and his hands folded meekly on the table in front of him. His eyes are red and swollen. He does not say much. But he does admit that his boxing career is likely finished, capped with a second straight defeat.

The meeting comes to an end. We polish up our bittersweet stories and file them to the country's four corners. A few of us decide to tour Montreal's bars until early the next morning. I feel as though I'm riding a high, hopped up on adrenaline and alcohol. None of us can stop buzzing about the evening's events, and with every drink it all seems more fantastic, better than fiction. Better than sex. The emotion was spectacular. The rush unrivalled. We stagger from our final stop, a pint away from a stomach pump. But I still feel like nothing can stop me. I return to my hotel room with Ouellet's foggy head and Hilton's wide smile.

Too wired to sleep, I think about what Ouellet had said at the end of our interview. What the fuck had he meant? "This power gives you victory." Dawn approaches before it finally comes to me — the trick to a life in boxing.

Let it give you what you need, but don't return the favour. Keep the trade unfair.

That power gives you victory.

Now I know.

The final lesson arrives with morning. A second press conference has been called, this time in one of the glass rooms of the post-modern Montreal Casino. The cool St. Lawrence River drifts toward the ocean just beyond an open glass door. A fountain also bubbles nearby. It provides a gentle soundtrack for the gathering. I scan the buffet that's been laid out for the press, pick up a danish and a juice, and find myself a seat.

Davey Hilton Jr. and his father sit at a table at the front of the room. The pair smile for the cameras and happily answer questions. "I'm on top of the world," says the younger Hilton. He adds that he didn't sleep well last night. His cherry-blotched head was filled with thoughts of glory. Dreams of salvation made him restless.

Elsewhere there is emptiness. A podium separates the Hiltons from the table where Stéphane Ouellet was to have sat. Not surprisingly, boxing's latest victim has declined the event. To hear his foe laugh and joke and talk about a suddenly bright future would be too much to take. He chooses instead to search his soul at home. The first fight sent Ouellet to the brink of retirement and Hilton on a belated quest for a championship. The second fight saw both men inch toward their respective destinies.

"My father always told me I could be champion," Hilton tells the reporters gathered around him. "But I got lost. I fell deep. You get pats on the back and everybody makes you feel like a hero. But that only lasts when you're a winner. When you start losing . . . you're a bum, you're no good, you're finished. That's what people always tell you." That, I think, is what Ouellet is telling himself. He didn't take the first loss to Hilton lightly. The second loss has made the buckling of his heart complete.

The fountain continues to bubble outside the casino. I turn to watch its dance as Hilton raps with euphoria. Jets hidden beneath the surface spit a continuous stream of water toward the blue sky, where the sun is large and bright. The rays of light give the water an airy quality and make it appear ignorant to the laws of physics. It seems destined to merge with the clouds. It won't, of course. No matter how eagerly the water seeks to defy gravity, every drop of it splashes back down to Earth.

HAMMERED

I board the train for Toronto later that same afternoon. In four hours I'll be home. I settle into my seat next to a window and look forward to a restful trip. Montreal's skyline grows distant as the train pulls away. The landscape melts. Trees and outbuildings soon replace asphalt and row houses. I know we've made good progress when Lake Ontario suddenly comes into view. Despite the low sun, the lake looks cold and grey. The water is calm.

The man in front of me is drinking heavily. He barks out the name of an alcohol — vodka is his favourite — to the steward and grows more belligerent with every sip. He begins to slur his orders and insults people when they pass him. He needs a solid punch. I've learned that nothing shuts a man up like a beating.

The train continues to speed along until we reach Oshawa, just east of Toronto. Less than an hour from home, the train passes over something with a bump. We come to a halt. The train is quiet for a short time until the conductor's voice crackles over the intercom, announcing a short delay because we've hit an object on the tracks. I look out the window. We're in the middle of an industrial park. A chain-link fence protects the railway line on both sides. I wonder what found its way onto the tracks.

The drunk man stands up and pulls his bag out of the overhead bin. He approaches the steward and says he wants to get off the train. The steward says passengers are allowed to depart only at designated stops. It's too dangerous otherwise. I think it's worth the risk to get rid of the git.

The man is not satisfied with the explanation. He grows angry with the steward. His bald head turns red. He demands that he be allowed to leave. The steward again refuses. The drunk man begins to sulk. He's little, but he tries to throw his bag back toward his seat with authority. I laugh quietly as the man sits down. Nice try, I think.

My watch ticks. Night has almost fallen. The drunk man gets up, paces up and down the aisle, and continues to berate the steward in the meantime. The steward tells the man to sit down. The man orders another drink. I can't believe the steward will indulge him, but he gives the man a short glass of courage. He drinks it down, is emboldened by the alcohol, and demands again to leave the train. The steward refuses. I grow tired of the charade. The drunk man looks for support among the passengers. An elderly woman tells him to leave her alone. He looks at me and opens his mouth. I give him a dirty look. He sits down.

A police car pulls into one of the parking lots on the other side of the fence to investigate whatever was lying across the tracks. We wait. The train has sat still for close to an hour.

I will the drunk man to stand up. I want him to look at me again. I want to tell him to go fuck himself. He'll call me on. I'll stand up and tell him to shut the fuck up. He'll tell me to make him. He'll give me a shove. I'll shove him back. He'll throw a punch. I'll duck it easily and come up from the inside. Put a fist into his gut. He'll bend over and gasp for air. I'll think about letting things lie, but I'll be shaking with anger by then. I'll grab the back of his little bald head and lift my knee into his face. I'll feel his nose give way. He'll cough and splutter. Blood will start pouring from his mouth. He'll want to fall to the floor, but I won't let him. I'll wrap the fingers of my left hand around his shirt collar and hold him up. He'll look at me through glassy eyes. I'll cock my right fist and throw it into his jaw. His head will snap back. His legs will go limp, but he won't go down because I'll still have a hold on him. I'll pull my fist back. There will be teeth marks on my knuckles, but I won't feel the pain. My eyes will focus on his mouth. I'll drive my fist forward and crack him again. His front teeth will fall to the floor, carried out of his mouth by a river of blood. His face will have grown soft, but I'll punch him one more time. My fist will land with a crunch. Then I'll let go of his shirt. He'll fall to the floor on his broken face. He'll be choking on his own blood. It will form a dark pool on the carpet. He'll see his reflection in the puddle. Tears will spill from his eyes. He'll gurgle every time he draws in a breath. I'll tune out the sound. I'll make sure my boots are tied tightly. I'll kick the fucker until he turns over onto his back, then drop the heel of my boot on his forehead. His scalp will split open with a wide cut. He'll try to cry out, but his shattered jaw won't let him. I'll drop my boot on him again. Another gash will open up. I'll grab his shoulders with both hands and pick him up. I'll smash his head into the hard armrest next to my seat. He'll be an absolute mess. He'll slump back to the floor. His shirt will be soaked through. A stain will form in the crotch of his pants from pissing himself. I'll laugh in what is left of his face. I'll stomp him some more. I'll stomp him until he grows still and stops making noise. I'll spit on his lifeless body. I'll say, "I hope you enjoyed your drink, you fucking pussy." I'll lift my foot again. My boot will be shiny with blood. I'll swing it into his face one last time. His head will implode. I'll have to step on his chest with my free foot to wrest my boot from his skull. I'll be breathing hard. I'll be splattered with blood. I'll wipe my face with my sleeve. I'll walk up the aisle and return to my seat. The carriage will be silent.

The train starts up again. The drunk man is quiet in front of me. He's fallen asleep. I order another drink from the steward. He hands it over with a smile.

★ 6 ★

PRINCE HARMING
★ PRINCE NASEEM HAMED V. CESAR SOTO ★
OCTOBER 22, 1999

And the street lights look pretty and bright
From the tops of the hills that rise dark in the night
If it weren't for the rain you might never come down
To your northern industrial town

— BILLY BRAGG, "NORTHERN INDUSTRIAL TOWN"

THE LIGHTING OF FIRES

My next fight town is Hockeytown. The flashy English feather-weight Prince Naseem Hamed is set to box Mexico's Cesar Soto for the WBC and WBO titles in Detroit. Should be interesting. Most boxing havens offer places to escape the violence. The whole of Detroit celebrates it.

Hamed, however, thinks Motown's an ideal gateway to colonial riches. His chances strike me as slim. Though Detroit boasts a larger Arab population than any other American metropolis — Hamed's family hails from Yemen — it's also the capital of Rust Belt blight. For three decades now, timid whites have fled the inner city for posh suburbs and gated communities. Entire office build-ings have been blown out. Fast-food restaurants sit abandoned to squatters. Whole blocks have been razed, and once-prosperous neighbourhoods have been gutted and left to serve as sets for crime sagas and post-apocalyptic thrillers. Signs even implore Detroit's citizens not to burn down the city on Halloween, as has become custom. Hamed says, "Detroit has been great. It's just like going back to the Middle East." Beirut, maybe.

I elect to bunk down across the Detroit River in Windsor. I decide that a smaller percentage of Windsor's population is likely proficient with small arms. But Windsor ain't no Shangri-La. My hotel room provides a terrific view of Detroit's Renaissance Cen-ter (five glass towers built during a moment of unfounded civic optimism), but it also overlooks a block of soon-to-be-demolished stores and apartments. Downtown Eyesore is a dead zone. Aside from packs of university students on the make for drunken sex, the city has been drained of night life. The only entertainment consists of two strip joints, a donut shop, a Burger King, and the Windsor

Casino, a half-baked effort to bring Las Vegas to southern Ontario. I spend most of my free time in town eating Whoppers and pulling slots with carloads of gambling addicts from Michigan. It's as depressing as hell in hard times. The cold wind howling through town can't whisk away the smell of desperation.

Still, a worse reek has descended on Detroit. Beleaguered city officials have latched onto Hamed's visit like pilot fish on a shark. There was a time, just as Detroit was once heated by blast furnaces, when the city and boxing looked out for each other. But heavy industry and heavyweights have since turned their backs on Detroit. Hamed's arrival, we are often reminded, will help stem the flow. Politicians believe the return of boxing will kick-start the return of everything else that has abandoned Detroit — the factories, the whites, the prosperity, the hope. A shot of adrenaline to a dying heart. They throw the bulk of their weight behind the fight, pulling strings to curry favour. Even the Stanley Cup champion Red Wings are bumped to free up the hockey arena, named after the legendary Joe Louis, for the match. Louis may have ended his life as a coked-up casino greeter in Las Vegas, but he once represented the best that Motor City muscle had to offer. Now an arrogant kid named Prince Naseem Hamed has been asked to remind the city of its glory days. Detroit is grasping at a man slightly larger than a strawweight.

The lead-up to the fight does not justify the early promise. Ticket sales are slow. There are rumours that the fight will be moved to a smaller venue, or that the house will be papered. English reporters wonder why Hamed is leaving behind a sure thing in England for a blind stab at American success. American reporters, not surprisingly, turn their attention to Mike Tyson's post-prison comeback fight against Orlin Norris in Las Vegas, which is also scheduled for this weekend. News from baseball's ongoing World Series fills the sports pages as well. Hamed could not have timed his arrival on American shores more poorly. He's a rowboat competing for dock space with tankers.

But by the Wednesday afternoon prior to Friday's fight, Hamed has secured himself a following. About 12,500 tickets, or 70 percent of those available, have been sold. Organizers begin to trumpet loudly the turning of tides. "For a fight in Detroit, on the weekend of the World Series and the night before a Tyson fight, that's tremendous," says a relieved Lou DiBella. He's signed Hamed to a multimillion-dollar contract with HBO, and for DiBella's gamble to pay off, he needs Hamed to pack the joint. Promoter Cedric Kushner, a hugely overweight South African, also has reason to beam with satisfaction. "It's the type of thing a rock concert might do," Kushner says of the overnight boom in ticket sales. "Not a boxing show. This is wonderful."

Hamed's trainer, Emanuel Steward — who still acts as counsel for Lennox Lewis — is especially pleased. He's as Detroit as they come. Steward longs to see his hometown's just-around-the-corner renaissance finally become a reality, and he, too, feels the Prince is the key to the city's success. He wants his pupil to move to Detroit full time, thereby serving a dual purpose. "Based on the tremendous support he has gotten here," Steward says, "I think it would be a smart move. He needs a base, and we need a local attraction. He would fill a void right now. That would be very good for him, but it would also be good for us."

Hamed speaks well of Detroit but remains noncommittal. Regardless, Steward feels the fight will put his hometown on boxing's map. "Detroit is going to be very healthy from a boxing viewpoint in the future," he predicts. "It's been dead. But now there's big money coming into the city. I just cannot believe the support we've gotten here. Especially when you consider that neither of these guys is American."

In fact, the only product of America on the card is the city itself, a once-proud metropolis reduced to the role of arena. Yet Steward's cheer is infectious. Hamed acts as though he's in the middle of a prolonged homecoming, and Detroit pushes Mike Tyson and baseball aside. Everybody works to tap the trickle of hope that remains in the city, using heavy bags to keep despair's flood at bay. While the effort still smacks of futility, the love-in makes me a convert.

I take Detroit's glow under a setting sun as a sign: red sky at night, saviour's delight.

THE PRINCE OF BOOM

There was once a post-punk band out of England called the Stranglers. Their music had a new-wave feel, but their lyrics were less optimistic. Before meeting Prince Naseem Hamed for the first time, I can't shake a particular Stranglers tune, a modest hit called "Big in America." It was meant to be sarcastic, a shot at all the bands that had fled the UK for a new England, a tongue-in-cheek suggestion you were nothing without stateside success. Should Hamed hear the song — a doubtful prospect — he would not laugh at the joke. He'd take the message to heart. Though a featherweight in only the physical sense of the word, he has long hummed a similar ditty in his head, haunted by the same refrain: "If you're not big in America. . . ."

In a sense, his Michigan mission is sad. Hamed's image graces stamps in Yemen, where his father was born. In England, the country of his own birth, the Prince reigns over a legion of boxing's most loyal fans. But try as he might, he remains a commoner in the places where it counts most to him: in New York, in Las Vegas, in Atlantic City. The snub hurts like a cracked rib. The cheering at home remains as loud as ever. But Hamed has a deep desire to fill the hole that America has left in his psyche. When he first crossed the Atlantic in 1997 to fight Kevin Kelley at Madison Square Garden, Hamed boasted to reporters: "I am what you need. I am what you need. Wait and see." American fight fans decided otherwise. A $2.5 million US advertising campaign netted just 9,000 filled seats. As many were left empty. Hamed later made a second effort as ambassador, but again he was met with disinterest. He felt shame for the only time in his life and vowed to erase it. Enter Detroit. Hamed hopes it will prove a carbon-choked Lourdes.

The final pre-fight press conference has been called at the

Renaissance Center. I take a taxi through a tunnel under the river. The entire Ren-Cen complex is in the midst of a serious renovation. Scaffolding and dust and plastic tarps are everywhere. Occupancy rates have fallen dangerously low, and the owners are taking a last grab at the city's hearts. Hamed finds himself in the same situation. He arrives at the press conference ready to earn our affection. A pink ballroom has been transformed into a bully pulpit. Hamed, a tiny man with a head of closely cropped black hair and a mouth of widely spaced teeth, doesn't wait to step up. "Apart from thanking everybody else," he says by way of introduction, "I want to thank myself for training so hard, for doing the right job. I'm in the best shape of my life. I'm about to put on the best performance of my life."

He soon owns the room. It doesn't hurt that Team Naseem, which includes Hamed's five brothers and his father, Sal, has left the audience stacked. "I can take any featherweight out," Hamed crows to loud applause. "There's only one winner, and you're looking at him. I'm blatant. I'm in your face. I tell you what's in my heart. Cesar Soto's going to lose like he's never lost before." The Prince pauses for a moment and surveys the audience. "I'm going to put the beat," he resumes, "into beating. I'm not talking about no points victory. I'm bringing my own judges and referees, my left and my right. I'm going to win in style. I don't know what losing is. I refuse to lose. I don't associate myself with losing or talk about losing. I've never dreamed about losing. I can't visualize myself getting beat, period. I'm a pure winner."

More applause. Hamed's abrasive act works. There is something attractive about his ego. He's rightfully been heralded as boxing's best trash-talker since Muhammad Ali, and it's refreshing to hear a little guy talk like a heavyweight. "There ain't another fighter like Prince Naseem, period," he says. "I'm very confident at beating every fighter on the planet at my weight. It's the way I've been brought up. I stand up strong. I stand with my head held high."

Boxing has certainly aided his posture. Hamed's life story reads like a tough man's fairy tale. His father left Yemen to work in

Sheffield's steel mills, places of unparalleled blackness, until he earned enough money to buy a corner shop. His mother — "the great Queen," as Hamed calls her — worked beside her husband in their adopted home. The business began to prosper. A penny's profit came with every packet of cigarettes or bag of sweets sold. With stability came the desire to build a family. The Hamed clan was not complete until five boys and four girls crowded the house next to the shop.

The children put in their time behind the counter. The work gave a young Naseem the urge to escape. At the same time, the Hameds took their fair share of abuse as Arabs in England's pale north. The stick made Naseem angry. His twin needs for flight and fight were met when Sal Hamed, tired of his children being taunted, took his boys to the local boxing gym. If they were going to scrap, he decided, then they would learn how to bash heads properly.

Naseem — already dubbed Naz by those close to him — was seven years old. As luck would have it, he was a natural. He was twelve years old when he told Harry Mullan, the editor of the *Boxing News*, "You ought to write a story about me. I am going to be a world champion." At eighteen, the Prince fought as a professional for the first time; three years later, he picked up the WBO featherweight title with an eighth-round TKO of Steve Robinson. Before his fight with Cesar Soto, Hamed had accumulated a flawless record of 32–0 with 29 KOs. He was a brawler with panache. He possessed unrivalled power in his left fist especially. An absolute firecracker.

But with his rise came harsh criticism as well as praise. Despite his success in the ring, Hamed's ability as a fighter is often downplayed by boxing scientists. He lacked an effective defence; his punches were long and left him off balance and open to counterattacks; his stamina was questioned; he could be distracted by his own hype. His arrogance also closed doors. People grew tired of his brazen nature. When he received his Member of the Order of the British Empire from Prince Charles in May 1999, the twenty-five-year-old loudly wondered why it had taken so long. The last good British heavyweight, Sir Henry Cooper, launched a prolonged personal attack in response. Cooper had soon mustered an army. Fight fans began to tune in with hopes that the Prince would lose his crown. But Hamed refused to indulge them. In fact, he became even more acerbic. "There ain't nobody else like me," said Hamed, who bragged that he would be the first unified featherweight champion and the first boxer at any weight to hold four belts at once. "I will be a legend," he tells his latest audience all very matter-of-factly. "I will go down in history."

The boast brings a bemused smile to the face of HBO's Lou DiBella. Before the press conference, he'd given a frank assessment of Hamed's über-ego: "Yeah, he irks a lot of people. But people have to understand that the Prince and Naz are two very different characters. Naz is a nice guy, a family man. The Prince is an arrogant little shit. But the Prince is Naz's creation, and it's a pretty friggin' great creation. It breathes life into boxing. I think he's one of three or four of the most important fighters in the world."

Even Hamed's detractors must grudgingly agree. America is still ruled by heavyweights, but the Prince has made small men — he stands just five-foot-three — hot commodities. "I broke the cashbox open," Hamed brags. "I've created an industry in that way. I've let all of the heavyweights know: it's not about your weight. It's about being an exception. It's about being a talent. I've proved that I'm something different." Hamed's contract with HBO is worth at least $48 million US. He'll earn $5 million US for his fight with Soto alone. The mountain of money allowed him to set up a virtual fiefdom in Sheffield. Through Naseem Hamed Enterprises, which employs all but two members of the Hamed family, the Prince has purchased dozens of properties, including his family's corner shop. He describes the excess simply: "Living large."

"He's created an oasis for small fighters," says Emanuel Steward after his pupil has brought down the curtain on the show. "Who would have dreamed of him making that kind of money?" Steward is right, but something about him doesn't ring true, and he looks stressed despite the prospect of an easy afternoon. I ask him what's up. In a moment of honesty, Steward confesses that he's worried about Soto, a veteran fighter who has never been knocked down. "He's a computer printout of the kind of guy that can be a problem for Naz," says Steward, his eyes never quite meeting mine. "You see, Naz fights a kamikaze-type fight. He's willing to get hit. I expect him to get hit. That's a definite concern."

Steward has reason to be worried. Hamed has tasted canvas more often than most undefeated fighters. During a fight with Paul Ingle — which he came back to win — Hamed's nose began to flow freely early on. His hand was broken, and he was soaked in blood. He can't afford to be hurt again, and Steward has taught Hamed to shorten his punches, to keep his balance, to be more alert in the ring. It remains to be seen whether the lessons have taken hold.

Soto, for his part, seems calm. He believes he'll win. He certainly isn't a light touch. Soto first fought as a professional at thirteen; he has a record of 53–7–2 with 39 KOs, and he took the WBC title from the difficult Luisito Espinosa. Soto's broad, flat face looks as though it's been battered but never broken. He's never been cut in his long career. "I feel very confident for the fight," Soto tells the room through a translator. "I know Hamed is a great champion, but he's going to face another great champion. I know I'm not the favourite, but I've never thought about losing this fight. The Mexican people, we are all warriors, and we fight to the end. I wish good luck to Hamed. God help him."

The room listens politely, but all eyes turn back to Hamed instantly. He simply smiles. He'll save his last words for the ring. DiBella is excited at the prospect of a good show. HBO has put big money into their slight brown hope once again. In New York, a massive billboard has been erected to promote the fight. It depicts Hamed arriving on American shores via sea serpent, an over-the-top display designed to give the boxer Yankee-style sex appeal. "You can do fun things with this kid," says DiBella, who acts a touch sheepish when asked about the billboard. "He just looks like a rock star." HBO will also broadcast the fight during prime time rather than the late evening, an effort to capture less traditional boxing demographics such as families and teens. The opening bell will be the earliest ever for a Main Event in America.

For a moment, the fuss suddenly seems to strike Hamed. He has climbed down from the stage and stands in a corner of the room, politely answering questions from a long line of reporters. He becomes something close to reflective. "I suppose I'm living a dream," he says with uncharacteristic humility. "My whole life is a dream. I can only thank Allah for all of it. I honestly believe with God up there pushing the buttons and me downstairs doing the business. . . ." Hamed trails off. He thinks about his next move, pondering rather than shooting from the hip. "None of this," he resumes quietly, "would be able to happen without God, basically."

Those within earshot are taken slightly aback. Was Hamed beginning to soften? Was the act turning into a hollow charade? Has his ego been damaged by Soto's bravado or America's apathy?

A local sportswriter, perhaps made skeptical by Hamed's switch in tone, asks whether this fight will finally break open American banks — or mark the end of Naz as we know him.

Hamed looks up. He stares at the reporter. He thinks about his answer. And he spits out a response with the tenor of machine-gun fire. "I believe I have all the ability," Hamed says, "and everything else to make me whatever I want. In life. In boxing. In America. I believe it will happen. I don't think. I know. It's just a matter of time."

The Prince will say no more. He leaves the ballroom. His entourage files out behind him. Steward looks at his watch. He steels himself for a workout.

THE KRONK GYM

Several taxi drivers wait outside the Renaissance Center. They stand in a clump near the lobby doors. They all suck on the butts of unfiltered cigarettes; the exhaust from their idling cars adds to the haze.

The group asks in unison where I'm headed. "The Kronk," I reply. "There's a boxing gym there." The cabbies eye me with suspicion. A white man best not go to that part of town, and only one of the drivers will even consider acting as my escort. Ray is a thin, older black man; I convince him to take me. I'm excited to visit Emanuel Steward's legendary factory. Some of Detroit's finest hardware has been forged there: Thomas (The Hitman) Hearns, Gerald McClellan, Lennox Lewis, and Michael Moorer. Now Prince Naseem Hamed has travelled thousands of miles to bake in the same furnace. One more champion for Steward's collection.

The taxi driver finds his way to Detroit's troubled west side. The Kronk Gym occupies the basement of a crumbling community centre. The neon sign of a liquor store flashes across the street. Most of the other nearby buildings are abandoned and falling down. I'm wondering how I'll get home when Ray decides to come inside for a look. He eases his old car onto a vacant lot. We step gingerly over broken glass and discarded tires until we reach the front door of the centre. We walk through the door and enter a makeshift games room. Two teenagers play ping-pong on an ancient table. Wayward paddles and inner-city tempers have taken great chunks out of it. Ray and I nod to the kids and head down a narrow set of stairs. A red metal door blocks our path at the bottom. A hand-painted sign reads, "This door has led many to pain & fame." An honest advertisement for a boxing club. A blast of heat rushes into the stairwell when I open the door. The entire club, a tiny sauna of a place, is immediately revealed. The walls drip with condensation and history.

Two dozen boxers and as many observers crowd the room, huddled among the heavy bags and exercise bikes and the club's single ring. Gangsta rap pounds from an imported boom box that's here courtesy of the Prince. It sets a quick tempo for the afternoon workout of this army of hard men. Sweat pours from faces scarred in sanctioned fights and back-alley brawls.

Hamed emerges from Steward's office and sits on a weight

bench. He bounces to the music as his hands are carefully wrapped and taped. He climbs through the ropes. Ten boxers dance in the ring, but they make like dance-floor fluff and scatter when the diva arrives. Fighters subscribe to an unwritten code of respect: status equals space.

The Prince begins his warmup. It smacks more of *Saturday Night Fever* than *Friday Night Fights*. He moves like a robot with funk. His shoulders jerk behind his hips and his feet as he shimmies across the canvas. He throws the occasional punch through the air, but only when the beat calls for it. The locals laugh and holler at the flashy foreigner. Ray leans on the top rope and bobs his head. "You go, champ!" he yells. "Yeah, baby! That's the stuff!" Hamed smiles at his newest fan and responds with a pair of phantom punches. Each fist flashes in rapid succession. The Prince possesses an obvious capacity for damage.

Steward stands outside the ring. He slips a pair of red handpads over his taped fists. He looks like a man about to submit himself to the dentist's drill. He climbs through the ropes and stands before Hamed, raising his hands with resignation. Part of the show, perhaps. The Prince continues to dance, but now he has targets to tap. He throws short, measured punches toward Steward. Without warning, Hamed puts his full weight — a mere 126 pounds — behind a punch that lands with a boom. The shock causes Steward to bite his lip. A second big punch follows. Steward's feet slide across the canvas as he absorbs the impact. Hamed throws one more bomb before Steward gives up. The old man passes the pads to a younger colleague. Steward shakes his head after finding safety beyond the apron. "I swear," he exhales. "That kid hits like a heavyweight."

Hamed continues his workout. The other fighters either stop to watch or go about their business. I take comfort in the scene, the sanctified sameness of boxing gyms. The bags and medicine balls and ne'er-to-be heroes, they're all as heavy as the water in a nuclear plant. The slap of jump ropes on the floor and speed bags on the ceiling makes for a familiar symphony. Even the whiff is soothing. Nowhere is boxing's romance more real.

I break my trance and cast a critical eye at the Kronk's stable. I've become better at separating champions from victims. There are a few pretenders lurking who seem doomed to a future of black-outs. Some guys show talent but do not yet possess marketable skills. And there are the favoured few — Hamed, yes, but others as well — who are the real deal. Their workouts have the rhythm of an efficient routine. They complete each task fully but without fanfare. Their eyes hold both desire and hate.

One boxer in particular: the dangerous Oba Carr, who spars with his shadow in one corner of the gym. He has the hood of his track suit pulled down over his brow. Sweat and spit fly from his obscured face with every jab and cross. He lets go a stream of mean grunts. I'm taken by Carr's dedication to himself, like Dale Brown before him. He seems unconcerned with today's chaos. The Prince is nothing to get excited about. The Kronk is Carr's place of work — he toils until it's his turn to clock out. The grime helps him turn a blind eye to the glamour.

Hamed soon finishes his own daily grind. Ray agrees to take me back across the river to Windsor. I buy a Kronk T-shirt, yellow with red trim, for fifteen dollars before we leave. Back at the hotel my skin smells of salt. I need a shower. But first, I try on my new T-shirt. It's as tight as a wetsuit. I need to work out myself. Maybe it's time to stop watching. Maybe I can find my own Kronk.

THIRTEEN OUNCES

Cesar Soto comes in a little heavy, too, and the weigh-in turns into a fiasco. The chaos is confined to a restaurant in the basement of the Joe Louis Arena. Dozens of reporters and hundreds of less neutral observers crowd before a low platform. Chairs have been knocked over and lifted out of the way. Elbows are thrown and necks stretched to gain a better view.

★★★PRINCE NASEEM HAMED UNLOADS AT DETROIT'S KRONK GYM★★★★★

For some reason, two scales — one digital, one traditional — have been set up. The stage is set for controversy. Hamed, much to the delight of his family and supporters, steps onto the modern model and makes the 126-pound limit without difficulty. He raises his arms in triumph when the figure is announced. Soto then takes to the same scale. He's thirteen ounces over — a pint of lager, a slab of steak, a baked potato with the fixings away from legality. It never bodes well when a fighter can't make the weight. Soto will have to sweat off the excess within an hour. He'll have already dropped several pounds in water weight. The exertion required to lose an additional thirteen ounces will leave him even more tired and dehydrated. He'll be a dried-out shell. The Hamed camp begins to crow. Their hero will conquer.

But Soto, no fool, jumps quickly to the other scale. It decrees him fit to fight, 126 pounds on the nose. An over-his-head official — remember, Detroit hasn't hosted a big fight in years — allows the second measurement to stand. Team Naseem cries foul. The floor erupts. The two camps go toe to toe. Reporters rush the stage. A huge potted palm falls over in the fray.

The Prince sees an opening. He seizes a microphone and yet another opportunity to grandstand. He climbs on top of a table. Two of his brothers hold him by the ankles. "What's it mean when you can't make the weight?" he cries. "It means you're weak." Hamed pauses. His face resembles that of a southern politician who has brought a rally to its feet and is about to bring down the house. "And what happens when you're weak?" Hamed asks, using his gut to push the taunt to the back of the building. "You get knocked out!" he replies. "You get knocked out!" Wild cheering ensues. Hamed nods, drops the microphone, steps down from the table, and storms out of the room. His foot soldiers follow.

Soto and his corner disappear behind a curtain. Even though they've dodged a thirteen-ounce bullet, the afternoon has left them visibly unsettled. The fight very nearly broke out early, and Soto has been exposed as unprepared. Hamed looks like the hungry one.

GET READY

My first fight of the night is for a seat. Joe Louis Arena isn't sold out, but it's a busy building. The Detroit police are taking no chances. Security is impressive. All in attendance have to pass through a metal detector and endure a pat-down before entry. Finally, I'm handed a ticket for a seat in the rafters. Not again. I refuse to accept the indignity, track down the man responsible for the VIP seats, and harass him until he agrees to put me ringside, where I belong. Lo and behold, I'm squeezed beside a beautiful Irish photographer — she has dark hair and pale skin and blue eyes and damn if she doesn't smell good despite the reek of the crowd. Only Cesar Soto's walk to the ring ends my rapture.

There are pockets of Mexican fans in the arena, but Soto's welcome is not warm. He climbs through the ropes with his corner and looks around the hall. He faces a daunting task. He sees the platform, decorated with black-cat sculptures and four metallic palm trees, that will serve as Prince Naseem Hamed's launching pad. He resigns himself to a long wait, pulling his stool to the centre of the ring and bundling himself up in his red robe. His face grows hard and his body cold. The delay angers him.

I don't know what to expect from Hamed. His pre-fight struts to the ring often last as long as the fights themselves, and I anticipate an elaborate production. Once he was chauffeured to the apron in a 1966 Cadillac convertible. Before a fight on Halloween, he bounced through a graveyard stocked with dry ice and pop-up skeletons. On yet another night, he descended into the ring on a flying carpet suspended from the arena ceiling.

"I put as much effort into my entrances because I've got people like you coming to ask me why," he told me earlier. "It's a big part of my career. I want to entertain people. I want people to see more than a boxing show. You've got to have big cojones to dance your way down to the ring, do a front flip over the rope" — another trademark — "and then try to knock somebody out. But that's my style."

At last, the Prince's latest extravaganza begins.

First come the Four Tops. Or is it the Temptations? "Get ready!" they sing with fitting enthusiasm. "Get ready! 'Cause here I come!"

They sing several verses before they're stopped dead by an explosion of pyrotechnics. Fire shoots out the tops of the palm trees. Showers of sparks fill the air and a blizzard of ash floats to the floor.

Out of the smoke emerges Hamed, still oiled from his warmup. He pumps his hips to the rap music that now blares from the arena loudspeakers and surveys his domain. The Prince shouts greetings into a microphone. "Yeah, baby!" Hamed cries to the crowd, which dances and cheers in response. "We'll have us a fight tonight! Oh, yeah!" Soto glares at his opponent from his seat in the centre of the ring.

Hamed, fully fortified, finally climbs to the edge of the canvas. Soto stands up and paces back and forth from corner to corner. His teeth press into his mouthguard. His dark eyes are now black. Hamed smiles. He waits for a moment, places his gloved hands on top of the uppermost rope, and flips into the ring. The gymnastics are greeted with more fireworks and loud applause. The Prince has earned the affection of his people with his early workout. But he's also found strength in his routine. He absorbs every drop of the energy the crowd offers. He takes the love and wraps it around himself like a shield. This is his party, he seems to tell himself. Soto is a visitor in Hamed's palace, a toy with which to play. There is no doubt the Mexican will leave on the Prince's terms.

But Soto does not look ready to oblige after the opening bell. Hispanic fighters are renowned for their courage and their powerful left hooks. Soto does not sully the reputation. After a messy first round, Soto catches Hamed with a solid left in the second. The blow wakes up Hamed, who goes on the attack. But Soto picks his spots and lands left after left. The hooks, combined with Soto's predilection for clinches and head butts, frustrate Hamed. He does not like to be hit. The Prince soon wears a mask of displeasure.

The third round descends into anarchy. Soto keeps up his roughhouse tactics, and Hamed falls to the same level. The boxers clinch and wrestle. The crowd grows restless. The pressure piles onto the Prince. His own hype has left him off balance and unable to find his stride. At the end of the difficult frame, he sneers at Soto and unleashes a stream of insults and obscenities. Soto counters with a smirk. Hamed fumes during the break between rounds. His smarts are submerged in a rising tide of rage.

In the fourth round, he finally breaks. He pushes down his opponent and wraps his arm around Soto's neck. He rips at Soto wildly. The referee, a sixty-four-year-old retired fire chief named Dale Grable, orders Hamed to loosen his grip. Hamed refuses, and Grable deducts a point. "What the fuck is the matter with you?" Hamed barks afterward at Soto, who shrugs in response. The outburst betrays Hamed's mounting stress. The foul puts still more pressure on him. Not only has his American invasion been bogged down in the face of an awkward challenger, but he's behind in the fight, too. Both his pride and his title are at stake.

Hamed very nearly loses both in a hideous fifth round. After an undisciplined opening minute, Hamed and Soto become locked in an intense embrace. Madness also takes hold. Hamed picks up Soto by the waist, lifts him over his right shoulder and body-slams him to the canvas. Soto lands flat on his back with a grimace. The fans, the corners, the writers are all stupefied by the artless manoeuvre. Soto's corner, which has been assailing Hamed with cries of "Chee-ken! Chee-ken!" from the first round on, demands the fight be stopped.

"No, ref, don't do it!" Hamed pleads. Time stands still. Emanuel Steward looks ready to burst beyond the ropes. Grable looks into the boiling crowd, his face creased with the weight of his decision. Fights have already broken out between the Mexicans and the Arabs in attendance. Brawls spill from the rows of seats and into the aisles and concourses. Downtown Detroit is not a happy place. Grable sizes up the situation and, not surprisingly, elects to pour a bucket of water on the hot spots. He deducts another point from a grateful Hamed but allows the fight to continue.

Hamed repays the favour in the sixth round, when he forces Soto to the canvas with another illegal move, this time a two-handed push. The Mexican jumps back to his feet instantly and implores the referee not to count the foul as a knockdown. Soto wants to keep his record of verticality unblemished, and Grable consents. Hamed then shifts gears. He resorts to more traditional tactics to drop Soto.

When he chooses to fight properly, the Prince shows considerable talent. He's quick and exciting, tough to read and powerful. He proves capable of grace. He's able to work his way inside, strike, and withdraw with an economy of movement. And he shows that he's a much better boxer than the plodding Soto. Hamed takes rounds with ease when he gets down to business. But the display makes his earlier theatrics all the more shameful. Had he been able to keep his head, he could have demonstrated his worth as a fighter despite an unfriendly stage.

The ninth round is his best. Hamed forces Soto into a neutral corner with a series of accurate jabs. A desperate Soto pulls his elbows tight to his stomach and brings his hands up to protect his face. But Hamed is able to penetrate the tough defence. He throws a strong left that finds a space between Soto's fists and flattens his nose. Blood explodes from the middle of Soto's face and spatters his chest. His upper body shivers from the force of the blow. His legs then follow suit when they wobble in time.

For the first time in his career, Soto looks in danger of going down. The crowd roars. Hamed presses his advantage. He paws at Soto's nose again and again. The pain from the first punch is made worse by the aftershocks. The Mexican's eyes begin to water and his mouth fills with blood. A look of sadism crosses Hamed's face. Here is his chance for revenge. Hamed's gloves repeatedly tear into Soto's damaged beak. He continues to throw iodine on the burn until the round comes to an end, saving Soto from further agony. He returns to his corner in rough shape, his eyes clamped shut with discomfort. It looks as though he'll need surgery to breathe properly again.

Yet Soto does not fall. He holds on for the last three rounds of the fight. He tries to win with a head butt, is penalized a point, and continues to hang from Hamed, who opts to jab and dance himself free. Though Hamed again shoves Soto to the canvas in the eleventh round, the rest of the fight is without drama. At the closing bell, the boxers are engaged in a clinch. A fitting end for a fight long on hugs but short on hurt.

Both fighters raise their arms in self-proclaimed victory before the ring becomes packed with officials and upset cornermen. The two camps jaw at each other from opposite sides of the square. Accusations are made and insults hurled. Somewhere beneath the fracas, the three judges give their scorecards to a man at ringside. He counts up the totals, scribbles them on a slip of paper, and hands the results to the ring announcer.

He declares that a unanimous decision has been reached. The crowd responds with cheers and jeers. Prince Naseem Hamed is deemed the winner. He jumps in muted joy and takes possession of Soto's WBC belt. Hamed also wraps his WBO belt — for the twelfth successive time — around his stomach. He poses for photographs with his gaudy treasures. He winks and smiles and pumps his fists: two belts down, he tells himself, two to go.

But the crowd is not so easily satisfied. They were primed for a memorable evening. Instead, they've been subjected to a card more suited to WrestleMania than championship boxing.

The night has been disappointing, brutish, and inelegant. But worse still, it's been uninteresting. "If I said it was thrilling, I would be lying," concedes Lou DiBella, who seems resigned to the fact that he'll never see a return on his investment in Hamed. "It was an ugly, awful fight. Sure Naz won, but he won ugly. Nobody looked pretty tonight."

The name of Joe Louis has been tarnished once again. The arena empties in haste. A crowd that was divided by loyalties is now united in chagrin. Soto's supporters will return home and complain about Hamed's bullying strategy and his flagrant fouls. Hamed's fans will wonder what made their man decide to embarrass himself.

And the writers at ringside? They'll sharpen their knives — or turn their attention to Mike Tyson, to baseball, to the rust spots on their cars.

We start our trek to the post-fight press conference. A reporter behind me taps me on the shoulder. "You think it was the Temptations?" he asks. "I could have sworn that was the Four Tops."

BOB ARUM PUKES

The press conference is as chaotic as I've come to expect. I drive my way through the crowd to a seat at a round table, where four or five other reporters pound stories into their laptops. I hate Friday nights. My deadline looms.

As does Naseem Hamed's. He and Emanuel Steward receive a mixed reception when they arrive and take their seats behind a dais at the front of the hall. Cesar Soto and his trainer — as well as his long-time promoter, Bob Arum — are already seated. They glance at Hamed in disgust. Soto holds his chin high in defiance, but his mouth forms a pouty frown. He looks like a child who's just been kicked out of the sandbox by his playmates.

"He is a paper champion," says the now beltless Soto through his translator, who repeats the boxer's jabs with even more venom than Soto likely intends. "In the real world of boxing, he should have been disqualified immediately for flipping me. A champion is a great fighter. He belongs in a pigpen." Hamed smirks at the insult, and the rest of his camp lets fly with a collection of scoffs and chuckles. But they know that an ugly, unspectacular fight was not what they needed. Deep down there is worry. Deep down there is a sense of failure.

"I can't honestly believe the way he butted me," says Hamed, who struggles to find an excuse to save face. "I didn't want to body-slam him, but I wanted to show him that he couldn't get me down psychologically. At the end of the day, you've seen my heart and character again. My heart is not like a normal heart. I'm always going to come out on top."

Hamed is mistaken. He won the fight, but he has not won over America. He's come up short on his third try. He will be denied his greatest wish.

Arum, who has engaged in a running battle with Hamed for ages, is only too happy to pick at the scab. He decides to hit Hamed where it hurts most: Arum wants the public to know the Prince is a pauper.

"I have been in this sport for thirty-five years," says the larger-than-life promoter, "and what I saw in the ring tonight made me puke. That is not boxing. That's clownish. That's wrestling. Name me a worse fight that you've ever seen. I challenge you. Name me a worse fight."

A little less than twenty-four hours later, there will be a worse fight. Even Arum would be hard-pressed to argue otherwise. Three time zones away, within the heart of Las Vegas, Mike Tyson prepares to take on Orlin Norris. The opening bell will ring and three minutes will pass, and there will be shame once again.

A full second after the bell sounds to end the first round of the fight, Tyson will hit Norris with a short, chopping left to the jaw. Norris will fall awkwardly and twist his knee. Chaos will break out in the ring. Corners and security guards will pile into yet another Tyson melee. After the smoke clears, Norris will return to his corner and be examined by a physician. His kneecap will be found to have been dislocated. It will stick out the side of his leg at an abnormal angle. He'll be unable to continue. The fight will be declared a no contest. Bedlam will follow. People who paid thousands of dollars for a seat will have been treated to 180 seconds of bad boxing — 181 seconds, including Tyson's late punch. It will be the second disappointing night for the game in as many days. "I really don't want to fight anymore," Tyson will say, still playing the role of victim. "I'm tired of this." The men and women who will file out of the arena behind him will no doubt agree. They'll likely vow, "Never again."

I've grown to accept the bitterness as well as the butterflies. I'm no longer surprised when boxing falls short of its highest ideals. It's a function rooted in violence: how much good can come from it? Fact is, it has always let me down. I've been left sad by Otis Grant, angry by Mike Tyson, distraught by Trevor Berbick, frustrated by Lennox Lewis, scared by Davey Hilton Jr., bored by Naseem Hamed.

Yet I'm torn. At least I've been allowed access to those feelings. My boxing credentials have filled me with emotion that I might not otherwise have known. I've become a man more whole thanks to the destruction of others. I've enjoyed a personal renaissance after embracing the primitive.

It's not that boxing and I have become close friends. Rather, I have met a bad influence who has shaken me from comfort and broken me out of my shell.

But like any bad influence, boxing has never had my best interests at heart. The game is always on the make. Despite my epiphany in Montreal, part of me still wants to come out of boxing's shadow. I just need to be made certain of my decision. One more chance, I tell myself. I'll give it one more chance.

★ 7 ★

A REVERSAL OF TRAVESTY

★ LENNOX LEWIS V. EVANDER HOLYFIELD II ★

NOVEMBER 13, 1999

I am fully cognizant of the decadence of the prize ring, and when I returned to this country a year or so ago after a long stay in the other hemisphere, I tried to drop it from my field of interests. But as I grow older, I am aware of a need for cultural continuity in my life, and in the train on the way out to Indianapolis, I felt the elation of a man who has said a lot of hard things about a woman and is now on his way to make up.

— A. J. LIEBLING, *AN ARTIST SEEKS HIMSELF*

A GLOW IN THE NIGHT

I return to Las Vegas feeling like a sailor who has just arrived at his home port: I'm excited, but at the same time, I know it will take me a while to find my legs.

I make my approach from the southeast, after watching Fall League baseball in Phoenix. I left the ballgame after seven innings, but it's still late. I'm on track to slip into Las Vegas at four o'clock in the morning, an hour of quiet desperation.

But I have a good ways to go. My rented car acts as a desert chariot, kicking up a cloud of dust as I burn my mark on Route 93. The dust, which has descended from the nearby hills, is made a darker red by my taillights. In my rear-view mirror, it looks like a windstorm has blown in from Mars. The lights from the occasional still-awake trailer home or taco stand form white streaks beside me. They blur with the combination of speed and fatigue. I roll down the window and turn up the radio. I don't want to fall asleep and drop into the Grand Canyon, which swallows up the world somewhere to my right.

Night falls on the desert harder than in most places. The sand absorbs the moonlight and takes it to the centre of the Earth. The beams from my headlights seem to disappear a few feet in front of the car, muted by Arizona's soft, shifting landscape. Who knew what lived just beyond the highway's shoulder? A band of desert hermits and scorpions and the odd cactus snatched from the background of a Road Runner cartoon. The blackness leaves me on edge. I put my foot to the floor. The sound of the engine grows louder. I point the car toward borderline civilization.

The desert eventually gives way to the frontier city of Kingman, Arizona. It is populated by an independent breed of people. I think about bunking down but push on. The odometer turns over. The lights of Kingman fade behind me, and I notice a glow in the distant sky. It floods the space above the mountains that separate me from Nevada, a ball of white light floating upward for miles before reflecting off the clouds, like heat lightning with no Off switch.

The glow consumes more of the sky the closer I get. I cross the concrete expanse of the Hoover Dam, its grey mass dotted with yellow streetlights, fireflies in the night. The greater glow, I finally realize, is Las Vegas. The heavens are acting as a billboard for sin.

The highway curves left and then right, climbs hills and tumbles down them. I guide the car around a gentle bend, and there it is. Las Vegas occupies a massive desert plain, and its entire expanse lies before me. The constellations have yielded to gravity. The strip pulses with electricity, and I'm instantly brought back to my previous adventures. I make out the bright green of the MGM Grand, the white of the now complete Paris, the gold of Mandalay Bay. The peace of the ballpark in Phoenix made me forget what stood next on my agenda. I remember now.

AGAIN

The rematch of Evander Holyfield and Lennox Lewis, in which the undisputed heavyweight championship is again up for grabs, has been billed "The Search for the Truth . . . Unfinished Business." A different search has already begun among the reporters who assemble under the glare of television lights at the pre-fight press conference: for a story worth repeating.

"Forget about the ides of March," bellows Don King, my old friend, to open the belated affair, held at the Hilton. "This will be a November to remember!" Flashpots are lit and fireworks set off to underscore the declaration. The room is made bright for a moment, but the smell of ash and sulphur combines to make a fitting stink.

Though King is likely right, nobody seems prepared to throw

their hearts into the ring lest they be disappointed again. Everyone has put the brakes on their hopes, holstered their optimism. Myself included. There is still a crackle in the air, but it's grounded by skepticism. The hype comes off as hollow. Even Holyfield and Lewis look as though they're going through the motions.

"I'm the undisputed heavyweight champion of the world," says Holyfield, who continues to deny that he lost to Lewis eight months before. "On the thirteenth, I'm just going to pick up my belts."

Not surprisingly, Lewis offers a different opinion. "Did Evander Holyfield just say he's the undisputed heavyweight champion of the world?" he asks. "You crazy," he answers. Lewis shakes his head, just like he did when his first fight with Holyfield was ruled a draw.

Excitement normally would follow the taunt, but only a flicker of interest ignites the crowd. After all, this debate has been heard plenty of times before. Holyfield-Lewis has been analyzed in courtrooms and sports bars and talk-radio forums ad nauseum. Though no conclusions have been reached and no closure found, attention has turned to other things. Namely, the stuff that haunts boxing's dark corners.

The man most interviewed this morning is Marc Ratner, a slight, bespectacled man and dedicated employee of the Nevada State Athletic Commission. It's his job to appoint the officials for the fight. Because of the mess that followed the first fight, extra attention is given the judges who will score the rematch. "We're confident that whoever wins the fight in the ring will get the decision," says a besieged Ratner, who has selected three judges from Nevada: Jerry Roth, Chuck Giampa, and Bill Graham.

"I'm not saying the only good officials are from Nevada," Ratner replies when asked about the wisdom of appointing three American judges. "But because of the nature of the first fight, we wanted officials we are very familiar with. They have judged over 220 world-title fights between them. I think this is a very important fight for the credibility of boxing, and we wanted our people to be there."

The often outspoken Frank Maloney, who was so dogged in his accusations after the first fight, is surprisingly agreeable. "The judges are very good, and we are happy with the appointments," Maloney tells a small scrum gathered around him. "But we don't believe the judges are going to be needed on the night." (The entire Lewis camp tells reporters to expect an early knockout, and Emanuel Steward says the fight will not go past the sixth round.) Someone asks Maloney about the title of the fight. "I don't think they should have called it 'Unfinished Business,'" he says with an earnest look. "I think they should have called it 'All on the Line.'"

For Lewis. For Holyfield. For me, too. The fight game needs a special night to keep me. Boxing's more loyal fans will be there once again — the 18,500-seat Thomas & Mack Center sold out quickly, and more than 6,000 translucent English fans have been deposited in the Nevada desert — but I wonder whether the sport will be there for us.

I expect the weigh-in, which takes place the following afternoon, to provide some sort of answer. Bundles of reporters wait outside the Hilton for a shuttle bus to Mandalay Bay, where the physicals are held. But the shuttle never shows up, and we break off into groups of three and four and hop into taxis. The fedora-topped Bert Sugar happens to be in my van. "Hey, kid," he says through his cigar, "how you been doing?" I smile. "All right," I tell him, feeling as though I'm talking to a ghost, a product of my tapped-out imagination.

We're dropped off at the south end of the strip. The media pack enters the casino's golden tower and storms toward the ballroom that holds the scale like a gang of thieving kids swarming a department store. Sugar tells one guy, who has the gall to ask to see his credentials, to fuck right off. The rest of us follow his lead, straight into a circus.

On one side of the room, a fairly large media contingent mingles in relative spaciousness. On the other side is a drunken crowd of English fans penned into a much smaller area. The supporters are jammed together as if standing on the terrace of an ancient soccer stadium. They chant and sing until the principals appear, accompanied by two buxom women in bikinis and a couple dressed as Caesar and his lovely bride. I'm not certain of the significance of the Romans.

Don King, his hair resembling the plumage on Caesar's helmet, emerges from behind a curtain to take his place on the podium. He's greeted with chants of "You fat bastard!" from the well-sauced Britons in attendance. King smiles broadly in response. He pumps his fist in defiance. For a few seconds there is quality drama.

Yet the reality is an almost complete absence of suspense. The two boxers are still fine physical specimens, powerful and lean and trim. But the scale confirms that Lewis has maintained a sizeable advantage. He comes in at 242 pounds. Holyfield weighs just 217.

Lewis proved in the first fight that he's capable of unifying the heavyweight division with relative ease. He's bigger and stronger than the aging Holyfield, who perhaps should have called it quits after his first meeting with Lewis. The eight months in between have allowed Lewis to hone his skills further. For Holyfield, the eight months have served only to advance his deterioration.

To make matters worse for his American foe, Lewis has also pledged to be more aggressive in the ring. He acknowledges that he failed to finish the job in March. Things will be different this time around. "I will not go back to Britain without all three belts," Lewis says. Politics and kickbacks aside, there is little reason not to believe him.

But there remains a tiny footnote to logic's ledger. Holyfield still owns boxing's biggest heart. It's a bettor's worst nightmare. He wasn't supposed to beat Riddick Bowe, to knock out Michael Moorer, to unhinge Mike Tyson (twice). Before each of those fights, Holyfield was deemed to be washed up. After each of those victories, his place among history's best was made more secure. He's asked to explain his heroic performances, and Holyfield says, "I would rather die than not give my all." Yes, much rust has settled into his thirty-six-year-old legs. But Holyfield is still alive.

And a Lewis collapse is not an impossibility. His own business manager, Panos Eliades, has used the word "tortured" to describe his career. He still has a tendency to fight to the level of his opponents, and he'll face tremendous pressure in the ring on Saturday night. It will be his responsibility to make people forget about the draw. Holyfield has everything to gain. Lewis has everything to lose.

"I'm the best in the world," Lewis says. "I think that my fight with Evander will open the door for my legacy." Defeat, however, would close the door forever. Therein lies intrigue.

Still, the promoters know an uphill battle for credibility remains. There are hearts not yet won over. Another press conference is called for Friday morning. A "shocking announcement" is promised. Rumours circulate. It's widely expected that both boxers will spit on the International Boxing Federation, one of the three sanctioning bodies involved in the fight. Last week, the IBF president, Bobby Lee, and three henchmen were indicted on racketeering and bribery charges. Federal prosecutor Robert F. Cleary said more than $300,000 US had been funnelled through the IBF by boxing promoters in exchange for favourable rankings. Should Holyfield and Lewis call the IBF title meaningless, perhaps the housecleaning that boxing desperately needs will finally begin.

The speculation continues until the start of Friday's proceedings, which comes after a ninety-minute delay. Frank Maloney and Don King stand together behind a podium. Breaths are held as they prepare to speak. It's time for the announcement, and they say it in unison: Maloney will run naked through New York's Times Square should Lewis lose the fight.

King then produces a red satin thong and leopard-skin bikini briefs — "alligator or tiger," he calls them — and suggests that Maloney might want to wear the undies rather than strip down completely. "Who would want to see Frank Maloney run through Times Square naked?" King asks. The mouths of the reporters present fall agape, but the room remains silent.

Maloney then wants King to promise to shave his head should

Lewis win. "No," says King. "My hair is a gift from God." King then produces a picture of himself from a fifty-year-old high-school yearbook, explaining how he needs no gel to make his mop electric, and asks for questions from the dumbstruck press. Only one query is forthcoming: "Why am I sitting here?" barks Sugar.

The jab hangs in the air. Other reporters nod in agreement and ready themselves to leave. The charade comes to a sudden end.

The stories in the newspapers the following day condemn King and Maloney for their foolish display. But the harpoons are thrown by shallow men. We all show up for the fight with smiles of expectation on our faces. For boxing fans, hope always springs internal. The dancing in my belly tells me I'm no different.

THOMAS & SMACK

The security guard pats me down and searches my computer bag for weapons and contraband refreshments. He then grabs me by the arm and directs me toward a metal detector near the VIP entrance at the Thomas & Mack Center, located on the south side of the city on the campus of the University of Nevada, Las Vegas. It's surprising that an institute of higher education is playing host to a heavyweight prizefight, though I suppose boxing has taught me enough by this time.

Lesson one: the bouncers still don't mean shit to me. I am permitted entry. I've already picked up my credentials. At long last, I have a very good seat that I don't have to fight for, one row removed from ringside but raised slightly above the crush. It allows me to watch the arrival of the rich and famous, forced to pass before me to reach their seats. Faces I've seen only on magazine covers walk by with increasing regularity. There must be more beautiful women in this arena than anywhere else in the universe. Trophy wives and starlets and hookers combine to form a blonde army of centrefolds. A cold front of glamour blends with a warm front of smoke. A nasty storm brews where they meet.

The English fight fans provide the thunder. They're stacked in rows close to the rafters. They've painted the Union Jack on their faces and draped flags across their shoulders. They're all shipyard haircuts and sunburns, football jerseys and livers swimming in liquor. Blue-collar Britons who've earned a four-day spell from the factories and docklands are dropping a month's wages to watch Lennox Lewis win the heavyweight championship of the world. They will not take disappointment lightly. Fortunately, they seem in good humour, their moods likely enhanced by England's win over Scotland in a Euro 2000 playoff game held earlier today. On the downside, the soccer match kicked off a dozen hours of binge drinking. The arena's upper deck is well lubricated. In a sense, I miss my seat at Madison Square Garden, though I'm probably safer down here. The first fight song breaks out at precisely 7 p.m., almost two hours before the Main Event. It's going to be a long night — even longer should Lewis lose. Thank God Las Vegas is a double-or-nothing kind of town.

The undercard is made invisible through the atmosphere. I watch the crowd on the arena floor shift about with giddy anticipation. Ripples of energy rebound against either end of the building. Ringside waitresses fuel the excitement with round after round of drinks. The barmaids wearing bras use them to hold their tips.

The privileged American fans cast bemused looks toward the English mob, which continues to rev itself up. Mocking chants rain down on the lower bowl without pause. I wonder whether the two sides will keep their distance as the night ticks away. Twelve rounds will tell.

Lewis and Holyfield finally find themselves in the ring. Both receive rousing ovations upon their introduction to the crowd. A taped version of "God Save the Queen" is played over the arena loudspeakers, but the UK fans provide an enthusiastic overdub. The Four Tops — there's no mistaking them this time around — offer a soulful rendition of "The Star-Spangled Banner." More chants fill the void following the songs. As they did in New York, banks of Britons point at their brethren on the other side of the building. "Lewis! Lewis! Lewis!" they cry. The friendly rivals respond with a touch more volume. The competition continues until the arena seems close to shifting from its foundations. Only the bell saves it from collapse.

The opening round is tight and tentative.

The second round sees a little more action.

But the fireworks truly begin in round three. The two fighters bury themselves into each other. There are wild swings and vicious combinations. Holyfield stuns Lewis with a right hand that would down most men. Lewis remains vertical.

He holds on through the fourth round.

In the fifth round, Lewis sustains a cut above his right eye after a clash of heads. He responds by running Holyfield toward the ropes. Holyfield leans back so hard that he topples toward the seats. He grabs hold of Lewis, who very nearly follows Holyfield to the floor. For a moment, both fighters are trapped in an embrace and balance precariously on the top rope. A wrong breath or ill-timed movement would see them both exit the ring's close confines: the spectators sitting under more than 400 pounds of rootless boxer see their lives flash before their eyes. Only the referee manages to rescue the dire situation. He applies weight to the feet of Holyfield and Lewis, and both men are grounded. The scare seems to settle down both fighters. The round ends quietly.

The sixth is calm, too.

But the seventh round is something else. It's filled with the best stuff that boxing has to offer. Three solid minutes make all the sport's cheap shots meaningless. Everybody, including Holyfield and Lewis, stays on their feet for the entire round. The action is desperate. Both fighters consent to furious exchanges. Lefts and rights batter heads and bellies. Holyfield seems unstoppable. He drives into Lewis repeatedly, coming up from the inside and letting loose with punch after punch. Lewis does his best to counter. He no doubt hurts Holyfield with a series of overhand rights. But it's Lewis who looks to be in something close to trouble. His legs are not as sturdy as they need to be. His face contorts with surprise.

At the sound of the bell, he finds his way back to his corner, but with some difficulty. I wonder whether he'll rise from his stool when the time comes for more action.

The crowd urges the fighters on during the break. Perhaps the songs and the chants and the cheers give Lewis strength.

He answers the bell in the eighth and tears into Holyfield. They're toe to toe. This time, Holyfield is left in a fog. Lewis ends the round with a flurry of late punches. Holyfield ends the round on legs that have lost all feeling.

Now it's Holyfield's turn to answer the bell. After the sixty-second timeout, he does. But Lewis continues the attack. He turns his fist each time he connects in order to increase the impact of the blows. Holyfield absorbs a terrible amount of abuse. At the end of the round, he looks to all four corners before finding sanctuary. He has been completely turned around by the violence. He limps toward his stool.

Both fighters are on the brink of exhaustion. It's a miracle that neither has gone down.

But rounds ten and eleven are muted by their combined fatigue. The fight remains close. I glance at my scorecard before the final round. The last frame will decide the fight. Three minutes will determine who will be the next heavyweight champion of the world.

Both Lewis and Holyfield have accepted that hard fact. They come out with their hands up. They tap into their last pools of energy. But it's Holyfield who claims the final frame. It's Holyfield who possesses the reserve most deep.

I tally my score. A couple of rounds are virtually even. I remember both fighters trying to steal frames with bursts of late activity. Both fighters have also been hurt. But I award the fight to Holyfield, 115–113. A close call — much more of a draw than the first fight — but the crowd confirms my suspicion. The English fans are finally quiet. They sit in the cheap seats with glum faces and sore chests. The American fans remain on their feet long after the closing bell. Saturday night's celebration has already begun.

Holyfield accepts hearty congratulations from his supporters. Lewis is consoled by his corner.

The ring announcer clears his throat. He brings the microphone to his lips. He says a unanimous decision has been reached. A sense of relief washes over the arena. There will be no controversy of the kind that followed the first fight. The first judge, Jerry Roth, scores the fight 115–113. The second judge, Chuck Giampa, scores it 116–112. The third judge, Bill Graham, scores it 117–111. Holyfield took more rounds than I thought possible.

The man with the microphone waits a beat for drama's sake. Then he announces the winner's name.

It begins not with an E but an L.

Lewis exhales and looks at the sky through the arena ceiling. Frank Maloney begins to jump up and down with joy. The rest of the imported corner hugs and holds back tears.

For the briefest of moments, the 18,500 fans pause to watch the celebration. The building then withstands a jarring reversal, déjà vu engineered by emotion. The speeding train is thrown into reverse. The English fans break free of their lethargy. They roar and wave their flags. They burst into song and share bright-eyed smiles and high-fives. The Americans stand with shoulders that have suddenly slumped and their jaws on the floor. They turn to each other with looks of disgust. Cries of "Bullshit! Bullshit! Bullshit!" fill the air.

In the middle of it all, Lewis is crowned king. At the end of it all, boxing will suffer.

The reporters gather in small groups and compare notes and scorecards. Few writers have given the fight to Lewis. Yet the three judges — appointed because they were both experienced and unbiased — have stripped Holyfield of his rightful victory. How did it happen?

In the midst of the continued celebration, photocopies of the official scorecards soon begin to circulate. The three judges have come to a unanimous decision, but they disagree on five of the twelve rounds. Two have given the final round to Lewis, though it was Holyfield who closed the show with a bang. And for Graham

★LENNOX LEWIS, THE HAPPY OWNER OF SERIOUS HARDWARE ★★★★

to give nine rounds to Lewis? We all agree he must have been watching a different fight.

It's fast becoming apparent how the bout will read in tomorrow's newspapers. The New York press, which still harbours great suspicion of Lewis, will come down especially hard. Boxing has been given a second chance. The fight has not disappointed. But the sport has stuck out its chin. It's taken the sort of blow that brings dark lights. A good night has been spoiled, a moment of glory marred, a bit of history tainted.

I can't believe it.

I've grown tired of bashing my head against the same wall. I've grown tired of writing the same story over and over again. I don't want to be let down anymore. I don't want to be here.

I WAS TRYING TO ASK A QUESTION, EDDIE

The procession of celebrities that passed in front of me before the fight makes it impossible for me to escape my seat afterward. Movie stars and professional athletes never travel alone. When the likes of LL Cool J, Andre Agassi, Catherine Zeta Jones, Billy Crystal, Michael Douglas, Bruce Willis, and Rachel Hunter get up to leave, it's as though a dozen rugby scrums have broken out on the arena floor. His People jostle with Her People, and the Ordinary People act as a buffer and fill in the cracks. The VIP exit, the precise one I need to access the imminent post-fight press conference, is as tightly packed as a plastic surgeon's office before a casting call.

I wait patiently for the bottleneck to clear but eventually decide to cut through the unmoving mass with my elbows up. The celebrities become mere obstacles that I have to overcome, speedbumps cast in spotlights.

I make it down the steps toward the arena floor, lower myself over a railing, and get swept close to the exit by the human tide. I notice Thomas Hearns, the boxer, standing off to one side of the stream, begging to be interviewed. Fuck it. I struggle to his side.

"Mr. Hearns," I say, "can I ask you about the fight?"

"What about it?" he says.

"What did you think of the decision?"

"I thought it was a fair decision," he says. "But you know —"

A man in a black suit then pushes his way between Hearns and me. "Thom-assss!" exclaims the man with great enthusiasm. "How are you, brother?"

"Hey, man," says Hearns. "Good, man. Good."

The two become embroiled in conversation. My watch pulls me toward the press conference, but I'm pissed about being cut off from Hearns. I tap the man who interrupted us on the shoulder. He turns around and I realize he's Axel Foley. Dr. Dolittle. The Nutty Professor. Mr. Eddie Murphy.

"Yeah?" says Murphy with his eyebrows raised.

"I was trying to ask a question, Eddie," I say. I try to sound assertive, pledge ignorance to his celebrity. Who the hell is Eddie Murphy to step into the middle of my exclusive with Thomas Hearns?

One of his bodyguards puts his hand around my neck and asks me to leave Mr. Murphy alone. He's polite but firm.

I forget about the courage time constraints can provide; I take a deep breath; I swallow my pride. I obey his command without hesitation.

The chaos has begun to subside. I drive my way toward the elevators that will take me to the press conference. A few reporters blaze a trail in front of me. Others are lifted by the wake I've left behind. We pile into the elevator, then into the room. It's not big enough to accommodate the crowd. There's at least one tidy scrap and dozens of chairs are tossed around. Why don't people learn that the chairs only get in the way? I spy a fold-up table close to the back wall. I push my way toward the pedestal. I climb on top of it. Two other writers soon join me on the makeshift perch. We watch as the heat of commotion fans all around us.

I feel removed from it all. Minutes before, I was trampled under the feet of celebrities, trapped by beings larger than my life. But in this room, right now, I stand tall.

THE USUAL

The press conference is an embarrassment. I can't see the participants, even from on top of the table. It's impossible to hear the questions, and the answers are muffled by poor acoustics and the white noise of a packed room. I try my best to pick out pieces of monologue. No easy task. Then again, how much can I be missing?

"Of course, I wasn't happy with [the scoring]," says Holyfield. "But I have to live with it." That's all he has to say on the matter. He accepts defeat with dignity.

Lewis seems more relieved than ecstatic. "It's a great feeling," he says with minimal conviction. "I always said that Lennox Lewis is on a mission," he adds, "and I succeeded with that mission tonight. I'm the undisputed heavyweight champion of the world."

His statement is not entirely accurate. One minute before the fight, an IBF supervisor left the building with the organization's belt — one of the three that combine to make the unified heavyweight championship. The Lewis camp had refused to pay the IBF's fee for sanctioning the fight. The decision followed the laughable press conference where Don King had twirled underwear on his fat fingers.

"We were trying to do the right thing," says Patrick English, Lewis's lawyer. "We believe that there is one heavyweight champion of the world. We just don't have the belt."

The disgust I feel makes my decision easy. I've spent a week in Las Vegas. I watched a good fight. I'll sleep away tonight in a fancy hotel room, wake up, file my story, kill the day, and catch a plane home. Then I'll make like smoke. I'll tend to more legitimate concerns, write other stories, leave the fight game behind. It isn't worth the frustration. I'd given boxing seven chances. They'd all come up crap.

The press conference fades to black. My experiences flicker through my mind like an old newsreel, like someone else's journey. I take the elevator downstairs and leave the arena. I stride across the empty parking lot toward a waiting media bus, the last steps I'll take as a fight reporter. Warmth falls over me, a feeling of relief. Of escape.

My year in Strangeways is done. I've served all the time I have to spare.

Like any good inmate, I celebrate freedom with a bender. It's late morning, sunny outside. I'm in a less-than-savoury casino called Westward Ho. The sort of place that doesn't cater to tourists. There are no shows or neon lights or cigar lounges. It's a den devoted only to chance.

The staff wear tight black pants and embroidered Western shirts. The pit bosses wear cheap suits and expressions that belie the desperation they've witnessed. The entire place reeks of cigarettes and spilled drink. The carpet is worn and stained. The interior lights hide red eyes. The blue sky can cloud over for all I care.

I'm at a high-stakes blackjack table. The other players try to size me up when I put down my money and buy my chips. It's important for amateurs not to share a table with major spenders. No poor play will be tolerated. But fuck them. What's the worst they can do? I'm going to roll deep into the afternoon, beat the system at its own game, and fly home with a suitcase full of green.

Things are going better than expected. Card after card flips over in my favour, and the dealer suffers through a dry stretch that benefits the entire table. But I'm not walking away when the going's so good. I test my luck. I'm showing 12. The dealer has seven. He'll likely finish with 17. I hit. He pulls the top card out of the plastic dispenser and turns it over. A nine. I have 21. Black-fucking-jack.

I laugh and finger my growing pile of chips. I'm a genuine highroller. I tip the waitresses who provide me cocktails. I bet big on single hands. Sometimes I win, sometimes I lose, but I always get a dose of speed for my troubles. The room is spinning. I play hand after hand with abandon. Bust. 18. 17. Bust. 19. 19. Blackjack.

Another round of drinks. Hit me again. And again. Stay.

My luck slowly turns. Hands I won earlier leave me busted. The cards I need lie buried in the deck. The dealer strikes ace after ace. Everyone gets face cards except me. My pile of chips turns into four glass-high stacks. My stacks become a single line. My single line becomes ten $10 chips. I've lost hundreds of dollars.

I don't stop. Push through the worry. My luck will change. It has to. I've played so well. The cosmos will shift back in my favour. Now. At this instant. I put the rest of my money down. One $100 trick and I'll be on my way to the Big Time, a blessed Benjamin for my empty back pocket.

I hold 20 on my final hand. The dealer shows 21.

BOUND FOR HOME

The plane banks gently to the right after removing itself from the runway. I watch the city until it's nothing more than a shimmer in the desert. I ease my chair back and sink into my seat. The setting sun streams through the oval window and feels warm on my face. It's been 365 days since my first fight, one day since my last. Time for a pint.

I'm not the only one thirsty for beer. Most of the plane is filled with English fight fans on their way home to London. The lager louts have convinced the harried flight attendants to hand over entire cans of beer rather than pouring portions in plastic cups. My seatmate figures I'm onside and gives me a can of precious cargo.

He's about twenty years old. His hair is cut short, and he has a thick scar on his temple. He came to Las Vegas with a half-dozen mates, all of whom sit nearby. They make for a formidable crew. They all look to have played rough during their rain-streaked child-hoods. I ask him what he's going back to face. A factory job, he tells me, in the city. He hates it, but it pays enough for the occasional splurge. The fight was his biggest-ever fork-out for leisure. Worth every penny, he says.

We talk about the fight. "Absolute magic," he confirms, though he knows Holyfield won. "Yeah, but Lewis got fucked over the last time round," he says. "So now we're all square. All even. We can go home happy now that everything's sorted."

He passes me another beer and falls asleep. His chin beats against his chest with every jolt of the plane. I sip my drink and search for bearable music on my headphones. The sun continues to direct light toward my face.

It's been some kind of trip — the whole year — something I'd never imagined myself taking. I met characters I thought existed only in movies and imaginations. I saw spectacle and excess. And I occupied a tiny sliver of space at that most fabled of places: ringside. Boxing asked me to ante up and then rewarded me.

But like Westward Ho, it also took my money and ran with it. The payoff no longer met the payout. I've made the right decision. It's time to cash in and take my leave. Fact has won out over wishes.

EPILOGUE

I try to quit from boxing straight up, but an old friend summons me back. Otis Grant comes close to death after his fight with Roy Jones Jr. Not because of the injuries he sustained in the ring, but because a woman somehow turns herself around on the highway in Montreal and hits his car head-on.

Otis suffers several broken ribs. Great chunks of skin on his upper left arm are removed by flying glass, leaving a wound that resembles a burn. His bruised lungs rapidly fill with fluid, and he very nearly drowns in the front seat of his Saturn.

I catch wind of the accident a few days afterward, when I read about the crash in the paper. The news floors me, and the thought of Otis spending time on a gurney makes me shudder. Another fighter on his last legs. Another boxer left for dead.

Several months pass. Otis recovers, and he and Betty are expecting their second child, a boy, on New Year's Eve. He again represents a dream story, the other bookend for my time at ringside. I'll write the Otis Grant sequel and bail.

I make yet another trip to Montreal. Otis welcomes me into his apartment, which is cluttered with boxing trophies and fight posters. We talk for a while, catch up. He then removes his shirt and the neoprene brace that covers the scars on his arm. Two large constellations of raised tissue mark his shoulder. They have been flattened with injections of cortisone, but they are still pink and tender to the touch.

"I think I'm the same person I was before the accident," Otis tells me. "But it did open my eyes. You know, you could go at any given moment. Something freaky like that happens, something that's not your fault. . . ."

The same way he turned our first interview around — God, so long ago — Otis brings us back to boxing. Remarkably, he wants to return to the ring. Only the scars are holding him back. "I see the doctors quite a bit, and they haven't given me the green light yet," he says. "But in my heart, I know the green light is coming."

I'm surprised by his desire. Otis doesn't need to box to earn a living. And he knows too well what hurt feels like. I can't understand why he wouldn't just walk away. Here I am, about to kick boxing to the curb because it leaves me reeling, and I don't even fight. I don't know the true taste of pain.

Until the following spring.

I'm speeding down the highway when I divert my attention for a fateful second and drive up the back of a car stopped in front of me.

The airbags deploy, driving my fists into my temples. My head snaps back into the seat. Dust and smoke fill my crumpled car. The hair on my arms is burned clean, the top layers of skin are removed, and I can taste blood in my mouth.

I don't see black. Just a shade of brown. The generator is running low. For a moment, I try to piece together the last few seconds of my life. Somewhere in there, I've been in an accident. I've been punched hard in the face.

It's a strange feeling, watching the fog dissipate from the inside out. Almost addictive, a prick of morphine. The flashing lights of cop cars wake me, but I want to know that sensation of pure shock again: heart stopping, brain crackling.

I'm moved to the baseball beat. It's comfortable. Easy. But something is missing, of course. I understand Otis now. I long to be jolted out of my box seats. I long for my car wreck. Like his memories of an oil-stained highway covered with broken glass, like the sound of the ambulance sirens when you're in the back of the van, it's tough to shake free of the savage.

I'm in New York, watching the Yankees play the Toronto Blue Jays, when I find my fix in Lennox Lewis. By blind coincidence, he'll face Michael Grant, an undefeated and promising young challenger, at Madison Square Garden. Tonight.

I break my vow of abstinence. I'm rewarded with a ringside seat in the same building that once saw me in the last row. I can slip back into a hallowed place and nobody will be wise to my defection. One fight, I figure. How much can it hurt?

Lewis dismantles Grant in less than two rounds. Grant goes down three times in the first round alone. He's overmatched, anxious for an exit. It comes during the following frame. Like a blow that stops time in a barroom brawl, there's perfection in the finishing punch. Magic even.

Grant is wobbled by uppercut after uppercut, and when he doubles over in a vain search for peace, Lewis places his left hand on top of his foe's head, cocks his right fist, and drives one more uppercut into Grant's face. Grant immediately feels his legs give out and lands on his back. After his body hits the floor, his head bounces off the canvas — once, twice, three times — before finally becoming still. He's counted out cleanly.

The youngster is soon revived. Brought around. He sits on his chair and swears at himself for his ignorance. He tried to attack the champion, but the veteran was too smart to fall for the trap. He made the neutral corner fiction. And he taught the kid a lesson he'd best take to heart: my friend, the ropes are there for good reason.

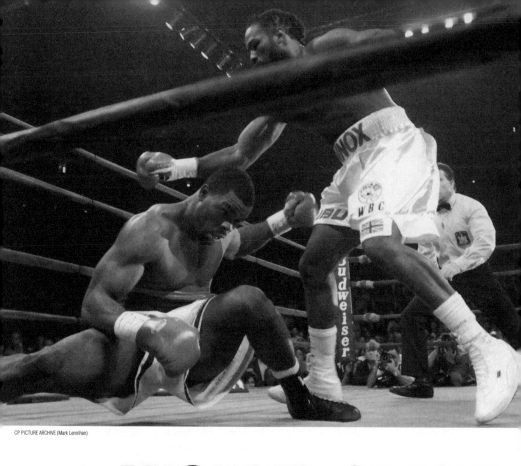

★MICHAEL GRANT LEARNS A HARD LESSON AT THE HANDS OF LENNOX LEWIS ★

POSTSCRIPT

OTIS GRANT continued to counsel troubled high-school kids in Montreal but was unable to box competitively after his car accident.

ROY JONES JR. became the unified light-heavyweight champion after winning a unanimous decision over Reggie Johnson, the former IBF title-holder, on June 5, 1999.

FRANÇOIS BOTHA suffered a devastating knockout at the hands of Lennox Lewis in London on July 15, 2000; it reminded observers of Joe Louis's fall through the ropes courtesy of Rocky Marciano.

MIKE TYSON remained trapped by boxing but began taking medication to control his temper.

SHANE SUTCLIFFE lost a second time to Trevor Berbick, his fifth consecutive defeat and the end of his career as a contender.

TREVOR BERBICK was forced to retire after a brain scan ordered by the Vancouver Athletic Commission found evidence of previous traumatic injury.

STÉPHANE OUELLET retired briefly but returned to fight Davey Hilton Jr. a third time on September 8, 2000; he won by unanimous decision.

DAVEY HILTON JR. recovered to claim the WBC super-middleweight title after winning a split decision over Dingaan Thobela of South Africa on December 15, 2000. Three months later, Hilton was found guilty of sexually assaulting two young girls.

PRINCE NASEEM HAMED was forced to relinquish his WBC and WBO belts for political reasons. He then surrendered his perfect record after losing a unanimous decision to Marco Antonio Barrera on April 7, 2001.

CESAR SOTO did not fight again until June 24, 2000, when he lost a unanimous decision to Oscar Larios.

LENNOX LEWIS was stripped of the WBA heavyweight title for fighting the unranked Michael Grant, and he lost his WBC and IBF crowns after being knocked out by Hasim Rahman on April 22, 2001. Lewis won their rematch on November 17, 2001, to reclaim the belts.

EVANDER HOLYFIELD regained his WBA heavyweight belt after it was stripped from Lewis; he won the vacant title in a controversial unanimous decision over John Ruiz on August 12, 2000. Ruiz won their rematch on March 3, 2001, to become the first Latin heavyweight champion.

CHRIS JONES continues to write for the *National Post* and covers the occasional fight. He has also joined a boxing gym.

ACKNOWLEDGEMENTS

I would like to thank Ken Whyte, editor-in-chief of the *National Post*, for the opportunity; John Fraser, master of Massey College, for the collusion; Graham Parley, sports editor at the *Post*, for the faith and the leave of absence; the copy-editing staff at the *Post*, especially Ron Wadden, for the headlines; Martha Sharpe at House of Anansi Press, for the support; all at Random House, in particular Rachel and Dani, for the attention. Also Lee, my muse, for making me feel like a champion. And my family, for all of those things and everything else.